Villages Voting & Taxes

Leif Youngberg

Published in association with:

Keokee Co. Publishing, Inc.
Sandpoint, Idaho
www.keokeebooks.com

ISBN: 978-1-7126-2289-6

For my sons Nik and Alek

Contents

Introduction

This is a historical political story, woven together loosely like a Navajo rug, sharing legends of villages, voting and taxes.

It's a profound reckoning of America -- "Old" and "New" -- inspired from the notes and Master Plan of my younger brother, Eric Youngberg (1967 - 2010).

"Old" America refers to America *before* the fork at Y2K -- before midnight of December 31, 1999 -- governed with a Constitution burdened with amendments, and a laundry list of silly "Addendums."

"New" America refers to America *after* the fork at Y2K --- beginning January 1, 2000 --- governed with just the original Constitution.[1]

---

[1] Somewhat paradoxically, as noted by a good friend who flew the Confederate Flag during his college years in support of States' rights, because "New" America is actually the *original* America, it is really "Old" America.

Eric was a popular state lawmaker notorious for "westside", "no doc", "handshake" deals executed with surgical precision. He passed away virtually in incredible fashion draped in a toga like Caesar, at the start of Barack Obama's 2010 State of the Union Speech.

After the police declared Eric dead, bloody and "bass-ackwards" in bed with his feet upon his pillow, his friends advised me that they had recently given him the new nickname of "Cire", pronounced 'Sire' or sī(-ə)r', the definition of which is 'father'. "Cire" is "Eric" spelled backwards.

His friends also advised me that they were helping with Cire's Master Plan to transition Old America, broke with a $14 Trillion deficit as a consequence of acting unconstitutionally, to New America, flush with a $14 Trillion surplus and acting purely constitutionally.

The two Americas (Old and New) had "forked" at midnight of December 31, 1999. Cire's Master Plan contemplated that at the end of the twenty year period from 2000 to 2020, those living in the reality of Old America -- a country perpetually at war, would begin living in the reality of New America -- a country at peace.

Lastly, his friends advised me to not take Cire's passing too seriously. Like many politically motivated events, they hinted that his passing was just another example of "fake news."

The book is a tribute to Cire. It is also a humbly appreciative acknowledgement of family, friends and neighbors who made great sacrifices in giving life to the story of Cire's death.

PART 1

Cire's Passing

"Never let the truth get in the way of a good story"

-- Preacher at Cire's Funeral

Obituary

1/28/10

YOUNGBERG --- Eric Andrew Youngberg, 43, passed away peacefully at his home in Albuquerque, New Mexico, on January 28, 2010. Eric was born in Albuquerque on January 26, 1967, and has now rejoined his father, Ralph Charles Youngberg. Eric was a true friend to many and loved laughter, whether by physical comedy or a well-turned phrase. Eric's keen wit and relentless logic allowed him to cut red tape with just a few words—he made casual conversations more focused, poignant and important. Eric worked as a real estate developer and investor. His passions included golfing, traveling, music, and art—Eric had an undeniable zest for life. Eric graduated from Albuquerque Academy in 1985, and received his Bachelors and Masters degrees in accounting from the University of Southern California. He also earned his law degree from the University of New Mexico. Active in his community, Eric served Bernalillo and Sandoval counties in the New Mexico House of Representatives from 2003 to 2009. Representative Youngberg served as Co-Chairman of the Historic Impeachment Commission. He was also an active member of New Mexico Amigos. Eric is survived by his mother, Janet Youngberg; his brother, Leif Craig Youngberg, sister-in-law Kathrin, nephews Niklas Ralph and Alek Charles; his sister, Kristin Marette Youngberg, and nephew, Erik Karl. Memorial Services will be held on Tuesday, February 2, at 2:00pm at First Presbyterian Church in Albuquerque (215 Locust Street NE). Immediately following the service, friends and family are invited to gather at the Albuquerque Country Club. In lieu of flowers, memorial contributions may be made in Eric's name to The Albuquerque Academy, 6400 Wyoming Blvd. NE Albuquerque, NM 87109, www.aa.edu; or the Explora Children's Museum, 1701 Mountain Road NW Albuquerque, NM 87104. Governor Richardson will lower state flags from Tues., Feb. 2 through sundown on Wed., Feb. 3 in honor of former State Rep. Eric Youngberg.

— Friends of Eric Youngberg ...

He was a true friend to many, and loved laughter ...

-- Uncle who spoke at the burial of Cire's casket

Political View

The above "Political View" was laying on the hardwood nightstand next to the bloodsoaked bed where Albuquerque Police reported Cire dead[2].

On top was an empty bottle of Nyquil® and the beat-up leather case for Cire's Blackberry. Cire had virtually lived on his Blackberry, orchestrating an almost unimaginable number of "no doc" collateralized digital business deals. Many had massive debt in default as a result of the 2008 financial

---

[2] The police report and evidence tied to Cire's death were irreconcilable. The written police report had Cire dying on January 27, 200**9** with his last text message being "**fever**". The police photo of Cire's Blackberry however showed his last text message was actually "**I'm taken ill**" sent on January 2<u>6</u>, 20<u>10</u>. Three things on the police photo, the actual message of "I'm taken ill", the date of 'January 26th', and the year of '2010' were all inconsistent with the Police Report.

collapse, the biggest banking calamity since the Great Depression almost a century ago. And now being upside down on enough loans to potentially capsize Vasa (Cire's international fleet of investment companies) and anyone else in deals denominated in Old America US dollars[3], Cire clutched his Blackberry and held on tightly until the coroner later pried it from his dead cold hands. That was how Cire's campaign manager Nick, the director of the New Mexico Film Office, had described it.

---

[3] US Dollars were established as the United States standard unit of money for *Old America* in 1792 by The Coinage Act (also known as The Mint Act), *after* the adoption of the United States Constitution. There is no reference to a United States Dollar in the original Constitution. The one reference to a dollar in the original Constitution (Section 9 of Article I) refers to a Spanish dollar.

Cire's friend "Art" who first reported Eric "gone."	Cire's friend "the Godfather"	Cire's friend and campaign manager "Nick" -- shown here wearing a pair of my Dad's boots while meeting with a professor of Art Law, Ms. Burr, a direct descendent of Aaron Burr who is credited with "winning the duel" in 1804 with Alexander Hamiliton, America's first Treasury Secretary.

The "White House"

The last time I saw Cire alive was September of 2009, at his New America "White House." The "White House" is where Cire was reported dead, first by the Police in January of 2009[4] (obviously a mistake) and then later by the same Police in January of 2010[5] (perhaps also a mistake). Cire had received the modest house, located just around the corner from his country club, from a golfing buddy as part of a *mandatory* Old America Treasury like-kind exchange[6].

Cire had moved his real estate office into the den along with a safe holding cards for lawyers, guns and money. He also had scored a truckload of cedar, which lights easily and burns hot, for his "Chimero[7]" in the backyard. I was

---

[4] The Police initially reported Cire "dead" at the White House in **2009**, right before Barack Obama was sworn into office as President of the United States.
[5] The Police subsequently reported Cire "died" at the White House in **2010**, during Barack Obama's first "official" State of the Union speech.
[6] "Like Kind Exchanges" are addressed in Section 1031 of the Old America tax code. The Tax Code *requires* that when certain investment property is disposed of, and similar investment property is obtained as a replacement property within a certain prescribed timeframe, any investment gain realized is deferred.
[7] A nickname for his fire-breathing portable Spanish clay chimenea.

in town visiting, having just flown in from Spokane, Washington. Cire texted, suggesting we enjoy the pleasantly brisk evening in the backyard of his New America "White House" near the fire.

Like most siblings, Cire and I enjoyed our lifelong rivalry. More than that though, we enjoyed our business partnership. We had formally established our Business Law Group in the late 1990's to capitalize on the eventual transition from Old America to New America, and consistently collaborated on making our business successful. We usually talked on holidays and met about once a year, except for the previous year when Cire had been more than busy entertaining re-election volunteers.

It was great catching up with Cire. We hadn't seen each other since he'd last visited my house north of Spokane a couple of Thanksgivings ago. That is when he, late in the night, effectively coaxed my pleased wife to join his political team as "public relations" director.

With Cire's 'red' Blue Heeler Tina resting happily at our feet in the grass of "White House" rose garden, Cire and I shared lighthearted updates at the fire from late afternoon until well past midnight. We talked and laughed enjoying a Dion's pizza topped with green chile for dinner and italian wine until the very end. Some of Cire's more memorable updates involved the following.

<u>Blackberry</u> -- Cire shared that he was now communicating with a few people using "virtually unhackable[8]" super-encrypted Blackberry PIN text technology. As an additional layer of security, to prevent the invasive Old America government from hacking into his private communications, Cire explained that the Dell® servers relaying his messages were in Winnipeg, Canada, the "Heart of the Continent," near The World Human Rights Museum. He then showed me how to step up the same technology on my Blackberry so we could communicate securely. We successfully tested the encryption and decryption with a few texts and then settled into deeper conversation in the backyard. We were just within shouting distance of the country club where Cire's mortgage broker, a handicap chairman and long-time friend of our Dad's, was then announcing that weekend's golf tournament winners to good-natured applause.

<u>Tribute Book for Dad</u> -- Cire was thinking about writing a tribute book for our Dad. He mentioned a proposed chapter on the golf clubs Dad had played with on September 11, 2001, when he scored his hole-in-one, an "eagle", and then followed it up on the next hole, against all odds, with yet another "eagle"! Before Dad passed away he had presented the set of clubs, which included a rare 1- iron, to a judge at the country club for retirement.

---

[8] Hacking was a topic ripe for discussion. It was going on everywhere. An email company I had scored the name for years earlier had just been hacked, again. Programmers, a contract one from Google and a brilliant 'coder' now in France, were pointing fingers at each other. The hack impacted our largest client who was also hacking us.

Other than that we didn't talk much about Dad's passing. It still seemed surreal, presumably for both of us.

According to our younger sister, Dad had passed away in the pre-dawn morning hours of election day in 2004. Surprisingly, when the polls opened up a few hours later, the first thing Mom did was vote. Anyway, Cire was contemplating options for a book about Dad and his hilarious sense of humor. We both grinned.

Vasa[2] -- Vasa, Cire's primary investment vehicle, had just purchased an ownership interest in a "mobile country". More specifically, it was a massive luxury oceanliner with every amenity imaginable preparing to "sail the seven seas" on its maiden voyage.

After Cire passed away I ended up talking with one of Cire's highschool classmates who had helped put the "mobile country" deal together. He explained that one benefit of the ship was that the "rules of the sea" govern. Under maritime law the captain may execute unruly passengers on board for good reason, or really any reason deemed sufficient by the captain in his sole discretion. The last photo of Cire before he was reported dead was taken at a Christmas party, with Cire smiling in his "Vasa" captain's shirt like he was heading for a cruise.

---

[9] Vasa is the Swedish word for "water" and "ship."

Last photo of Cire, in his Vasa captain's shirt

RV Park - Soon after Dad passed away Cire jumped into business with the Barr brothers, a trio of Native American football players. Their originally stated plan was to create and maintain a network of "high-end" recreational vehicle parks within a day's drive of each other on the western half[10] of the continent.

Many years ago the business had obtained a loan to build an RV park west of Albuquerque, New Mexico in a Spanish Land Grant, on Navajo Nation land. Plans changed and the business ended up building a "Texas-sized" RV park a few hours to the east, near the renowned Cadillac Ranch, instead.

| Cadillac Ranch | "High end" RV Park |

---

[10] Even though it is a bit further east than the actual halfway mark of America, the Mississippi River is generally accepted as dividing "west and east."

Cire had recently punted on the RV business at the majority owner's request. To accommodate the closing of the unorthodox business deal, which included a mandatory Old America like-kind Treasury exchange, Cire ended up trading investment houses with a Barr brother. That is how Cire ended up with his New America "White House" where we were now having pizza in the backyard in front of the fire.

Constructed on both sides of the line separating two narrow historic agriculture tracts, the house was about half the size of the investment house had Cire traded away -- and had half the value. And, unlike his previous house which Cire owned free and clear, the "White House" was encumbered with a mortgage greater than its value. In other words the "White House" was "underwater" and Cire had just "cashed in." This was confirmed with his laugh and disclosure of an additional house he obtained in the trade to boot - a sprawling, yet dilapidated, adobe territorial hacienda in a vast apple orchard.[11] Ripe for development, it was near the Rio Grande separating west and east in his voting district.

Elections

Cire had been elected State Representative for his district in 2000 and re-elected easily every election thereafter until 2008 when there was a

---

[11] The apple orchard, with its expansive gardens, had already been slated by his campaign manager, the director of the New Mexico Film Office, as the site for a movie about the Garden of Eden.

"dispute." Cire's opponent was claiming to have won. Cire was silent on the matter of his local election yet eager to discuss national Presidential elections.

More on elections later.

Constitutional History Update -- Cire was a big believer in the merits of "just the original" Constitution. He understood that the Constitution could be "amended" yet, like Thomas Jefferson, was firmly opposed to anything ever being "addended" to it. In his opinion America, and all of her citizens, would be much better off in the long run without any silly "Addendums," like the Bill of Rights, which had consistently proven themselves overtime to restrict, not protect, individual liberties.

As part of his twenty year Master Plan to transition Old America (with a Constitution burdened with a bunch of vague and nonsensical Addendums) to New America (governed with just the original Constitution), Cire had embarked on a self study of the Constitution, and wanted to provide me with the following updates on his latest findings.

- **Currency** - There is no constitutional requirement that the national currency of the United States be a "dollar." Indeed there is no reference to a US dollar anywhere in the Constitution, as it was only "conceived" of a few years *after* the Constitution had

been inked. In other words, the national currency of New America "could" be a dollar, or it could be almost anything else, including a new form of cryptocurrency that Cire was working on with friends to enable "every bit in the blockchain" to be tracked for a more sustainable economy.

- **Pledge of Allegiance** - The Pledge of Allegiance was, and in some places still is, an American militaristic ritual imposed upon impressionable grade schoolers. It requires that youngsters stand erect like a Nazi soldier, place their right hand over their heart and then babble some ancient poem to the satisfaction of the teacher. If a student fails to complete it just right, if they happen to wobble just a bit in stance or in prose, the unforgiving teacher is tasked with slapping the student's knuckles with a wooden ruler.

  This had always been a sore spot with Cire. In grade school Cire's nickname was "bloody knuckles" for the reason that his recitals of the Pledge of Allegiance consistently failed to meet his teacher's rigid standards. Cire was beaming now with joy, and raised his scarred hands in jubilation, to announce he had conclusively confirmed there was <u>no</u> Pledge of Allegiance in the Constitution!

- **American Flag** - Old America's "red white and blue" flag -- which the military has flown for more than two hundred years while engaging in war and conquering land -- is well known. The flag has changed from having 13 stars (one for each colony) to 48 stars (one for each contiguous state on the continent of America, after the Native American Nations were effectively disregarded) to 50 stars (one for each state, including Hawaii in the middle of the Pacific ocean). Just like with the Pledge of Allegiance, there is no mention of any flag in the Constitution -- much less a red, white and blue one, with an ever-changing bunch of stars[12].

Cire was happy about this for the reason it meant that New America could have "no flag" or, if its citizens so decided, a completely new one. No longer would "free" Americans be "forced" upon threat of bloodshed to pledge allegiance to a flag associated with more than two centuries of immoral wars and countless deaths. Cire suggested it was almost time to "retire" Old America's "red white and blue" flag in a dignified ceremony.

- **"United States of <u>America</u>"** - This is a big one. The Constitution does not contain any limits on the number of states in America. There

---

[12] As a practical matter, having a "timeless" flag with a fixed number of stars representing the States, which are bound to change and indeed have changed in number over time, is braindead. America can have as few, or as many, states as its Citizens decide. The flag, if there is one, should be flexible enough to accommodate a change in the number of states without constantly having to "re-do" its logo.

can be just a few states, or an unlimited number of them. Theoretically there could be hundreds, or even thousands of states all the way from Patagonia in the far south of America to Alaska in the far north of America. The only limit is a geographical one, which establishes that states are supposed to be from <u>America</u>. In other words, an island out in the middle of the Pacific ocean, like Hawaii, is technically not eligible to be a state according to the Constitution.

- **Surveillance** -- Cire was increasingly concerned with the United States Government monitoring its citizens. Given new military advancements in listening technology, increasingly fast super-computers, and massive relational databases, it was now possible for the government to hack into, monitor and record almost every electronic communication from every US citizen, no matter where situated in the world[13]. And, it was happening. The only exceptions seemed to be communications that were sufficiently encrypted, like those now on our respective blackberries.

Cire shared that there was nothing explicit or even implicit in the Constitution, or its Addendums, that gave the US Government the

---

[13] Somewhat ironically, much of this invasive and unconstitutional surveillance was being managed from Hawaii (according to a CIA operative named Edward Snowden who later disclosed the activities in his best-selling auto-biography). Hawaii, like the surveillance itself, is technically not authorized by the terms of the Constitution.

right to monitor its citizens. The fact the government was doing so seemed problematic. The country had already concluded years ago, during the Watergate era, that the monitoring citizens was an impeachable offense for the President. Now, as a flagrant violation of the right to privacy, in addition to monitoring electronic communications, the US government was monitoring private conversations of individuals in their very own homes, and backyards. It may have just been a coincidence but at that very instant Cire's ice maker, in the freezer of his kitchen, made a huge grumbling sound, almost as if it was listening, and trying to tell us something.

Cire grinned. Then he explained that there was nothing in the Constitution about an FBI (where our grandfather had once worked), a CIA (reportedly in charge of much of the monitoring) or NSA (which was known to be pushing the limits of surveillance by hacking into private company affairs, like those of Google, and even electronic appliances, like refrigerators).

Cire understood, supported, and rationalized the legitimacy of a Secret Service to protect Presidents --- past, present and future. He was increasingly convinced however that all the other expensive and unconstitutional "alphabet soup" agencies (like the FBI, CIA, NSA, EPA, CFPB, BATF, IRS, etc.) caused more harm than good, were annihilating Americans' individual liberties, and should be disbanded as soon as possible.

Cire also hinted that he had heard from reliable sources that my @ragnaar account on Twitter, promoting the human rights goal of unlocking everyone incarcerated for "free speech violations" at GITMO and everywhere else had prompted an unconstitutional following.

Twitter

Twitter was the last topic we discussed that night.

Since the earliest of times, democracies (and marketing) have evolved with order-of-magnitude improvements in communications, each being exponentially better than what existed previously. Specifically each of the following radically and profoundly increased the distribution of information.

- Slate (Moses' Commandments)
- Paper
- Telegraph
- Radio
- Television
- Email
- Internet
- Twitter #

Each forever changed the world. Sequentially they advanced communication from "one-to-one" (or "zero-to-one" for biblical purists) with the Slate, to "one to virtually everyone" with Twitter.

At that time Twitter was almost unimaginably more powerful than any other method of public communication previously known to humankind[14]. The potential with Twitter seemed virtually limitless.

The night of Cire's and my last visit a majority (now it is a "super majority") of the people on the planet had access to mobile phones and could potentially interact with Twitter. Increasingly almost everyone could frictionlessly communicate with everyone. The world would never be the same. The theoretical notion of a "global collective consciousness" was on a fast track to becoming reality. The best ideas could spread across the planet at lightspeed -- and many already were.

About a year before my last visit with Cire, a friend[15] from Portland, Oregon had suggested that I try Twitter. I did, and was stunned. Upon first signing in I saw "lightning bolts" understanding how Twitter, with radical disruptive technology, could potentially connect everyone in the world better than anything ever before.

---

[14] Somewhat disappointingly, prior to publication of this book Twitter "dumb downed" its platform, scaling it back to an increasingly repugnant highly-censored bland blob of trivial regurgitation.

[15] A "thought leader" credited with the prodigious thesis of "rivers and lakes should have water clean enough to drink" and Herculean efforts towards making that a reality.

Evaluating Twitter I was increasingly impressed with its simply profound platform and was tweeting a lot. Most of the tweets were for "pro bono" volunteer projects about the following -- all ideas credited to brilliantly wise mentors to whom I am forever appreciative.

- Protect and Defend the Constitution (#Done)
- Promote Free Speech (#CloseGitmo)
- Save the World (#EndTheWars)

Tweets were published from various parody accounts, primarily a "locked one" named @ragnaar. Only a small group of followers, including a couple of Senators[16] were authorized to view tweets from @ragnaar. The weekend *before* Barack Obama was sworn in as President with his oaths[17], @ragnaar engaged in a thunderous tweetstorm promoting the above goals and, ironically, attracted a following of unconstitutional parties concerned with the content of @ragnaar's tweets.

---

[16] Senator Schumer from New York, and Senator Grassley from Iowa, both of whom had taken an oath to "protect and defend the Constitution."
[17] In January of 2009, Supreme Chief Justice Roberts administered the Presidential Oath of Office <u>twice</u> to Barack Obama. Although there are different theories as to "why" two oaths were administered, the prevailing logic seems to be that one Oath was for Old America and one was for New America. Thus, Barack had the challenging task of being in charge of both Americas simultaneously.

The next few days and weeks, and eventually all of Barack's presidency, were a bit surreal. While @ragnaar continued to tweet suggestions to advance the above goals along with countless parties including rock n' roll stars[18], Barack Obama gave *direct orders* to accomplish the same.

Barack's first *written executive order* as President was to "Close Gitmo." He reiterated the order verbally countless times. Amazingly, his abortive troops simply refused to follow commands and, thus, were increasingly guilty of insubordination, and possibly even Treason.

Another bizarre anomaly of Barack Obama's presidency involved wars overseas, specifically the one in Afghanistan that had been going on since just after the events of September 11, 2001. Barack had been elected on the

---

[18] A special thanks to Bruce Springsteen, "The Boss," whose leadership and concerts helped inspire some of @ragnaars more memorable tweetstorms.

platform of "ending the wars." And, as Commander in Chief, he had the authority, power and responsibility to accomplish that goal. Incredibly, it didn't happen. America was at war (in Afghanistan and other lesser known places) when Barack rolled into the White House, and still at war when he rolled out.

Threaded through @ragnaar's ongoing tweetstorms, which continued from the suspenseful weekend before Barack became President in 2009 until Twitter locked @ragnaar's account in 2019, was a metaphorical suggestion to end the wars by "Turning The Boat Around." This pragmatic idea, first credited to the Swedish and later to Barack Obama, was worthy of a Nobel Peace Prize.

Centuries ago the Scandinavian Viking economy had converted from one at war to one at peace with a top-heavy Swedish warship named Vasa -- the namesake of Cire's fleet of investment companies. It had toppled over and capsized on its  maiden voyage. The upside-down sunken boat was recovered from the bottom of the harbor. It was then turned around, renovated and now serves as a maritime museum in the center of Stockholm's thriving arts district.

@ragnaar suggested that America, and indeed all warring countries, would be better off by transforming their economies from war to peace, like the Swedes had successfully done, by turning *their* boats around. Rather than send battalions of soldiers overseas for war, to needlessly have some warrior's limbs blown off and other soldiers die, countries could encourage tourists to peacefully travel overseas for education and recreation.

With the evening winding down, Cire brought up Twitter. Like a tweet, with a 140-character limit in the good ole days, our closing conversation was succinct:

Cire: Twitter is the future

Me: #HashTagVasa

Cire: Here are the #'s

After sending me a spreadsheet full of hashtags[19] which arrived instantaneously via a Blackberry text, Cire savored a last sip of deep-red Chianti poured from the now-finished fiasco. He then restated what we both already knew -- "Twitter has already changed the world forever."

---

[19] Some of the hashtags had already been woven into the twitter account for @ragnaar and few other affiliated accounts. Others would soon follow.

After that we bid farewell.

That was the last time I saw Cire alive.

4

Thanksgiving

Thanksgiving of 2009 Cire called. He alerted me that he was having "the pool table" (a century-old heavy Brunswick© from our grandfather) refinished and would be sending it to me soon. Cire offered a reminder that the legendary table was from a different era of America. The first games were played on it when women were understood, although mistakenly so, to not

vote[20]. Over the course of the next few weeks, the proposed pool table exchange was confirmed with texts and calls.

---

[20] Technically, of course, women (and all other "People") have been able to participate in elections since the Constitution was first ratified in the late 1700's. The Constitution specifically provides in Article I that "The House of Representatives shall be composed of Members chosen every second Year by the People...[emphasis added]" The Addendum adopted in 1920 sometimes credited with providing the women the right to vote was, and is, unneeded, superfluous and redundant.

In its earliest days, the pool table was one of two twin pool tables at a dusty ole Mexican cantina in Corrales village on the outskirts of Albuquerque. When the cantina's owner decided to free up more bar space for its patrons about a half-century later, our grandfather purchased one of the tables. It had been passed around among friends and family for decades. Cire had the pool table now and wanted to "gift it to me" for Christmas even though it wouldn't actually be delivered until a few months later, after the refinishing was complete, about Easter.

5

Christmas

During the Christmas season before Cire passed away he attended the traditional holiday parties and was doing great. We talked on the phone several times.

On one occasion Cire shared that he had just traded golf clubs with a friend, a left-handed bank president who was "getting hassled" by the Federal Reserve over Cire's "paperless loans." An army of bank-regulatory agents had recently circled the banker's main office with big black Suburbans and demanded to audit paperwork that did not exist. Afterwards, the banker thoughtfully emailed Cire a hilarious video of an Old America gas-guzzling SUV, complete with a red bow from Santa, being blown up for one of our New America pre-IPO investments for FUV[21].

---

[21] FUV is the stock ticker symbol for Arcimoto, Inc., the maker of the ultra-efficient three-wheeled electric "Fun Utility Vehicle," designed to displace most petroleum vehicles.

Other than that, most of the Christmas season conversations were primarily about the pool table, and how much things had changed since the first games were played on it about a century ago.

Cire reminded me that 100 years ago there were no "world wars" "income taxes" or even "federal reserve notes" ("dollars")[22], all of which are interrelated. Cire smugly pointed out that people now used their dollars (increasingly known as "petro dollars") to pay unconstitutional income taxes to fund immoral wars all over the world. Most recently many of the wars had been, at their core, about petroleum and rights to crude oil.

Cire then noted that oil, which started being burned in vehicles last century, was the culprit for polluting the air with exhaust. Next he reminded me that oil was also the offender responsible for trashing the earth with plastic, after it had been molded into disposable, but not degradable, consumer products and packaging. Lastly Cire commented that Santa Claus, who gained popularity about the same time as oil and the income tax, was the primary

---

[22] The Federal Reserve was "created" in 1913. Prior to its creation, there were of course no Federal Reserve notes. These notes, now accepted virtually universally on all the continents, are effectively a "one world currency." There is nothing in the Constitution about a Federal Reserve, its notes or US dollars.

driver distributing monstrous amounts of crappy oil-based plastic products all over the planet.

It was Cire's opinion, and a foundation for New America, that the world would be more peaceful, and much cleaner, without any of them. In other words, no more world wars, income taxes, federal reserve, "petro dollars," exhaust, plastics or Santa. Cire was striving for a peaceful and clean planet, just like God had initially created and that existed before "humans screwed everything up" to the detriment of themselves and every other living creature.

The solution, Cire reiterated, was for America to simply "start over." America needed to get rid of the Constitution's amendments and Addendums, all the chaotic aftermath and its toxic system of consumerism. America needed to be "reborn."

Birthday
(January 26)

Cire's 43rd birthday was January 26, 2010. I called and wished him a happy birthday. We traded updates and Cire mentioned he had a "cold."

We both chuckled after I mentioned an inside joke that "lots of green chili" would help him get better[23].

---

[23] Of course, one has to be careful with the green chili of New Mexico. Some of it is so hot that it can actually cause internal bleeding.

7

Death Dates
(January 26 to 28)

The precise date that Cire supposedly died remains uncertain, but it seems to have been either January 26, 27 or 28. The support for each date follows.

- **January 26** -- The mannered lawyers and languid probate Judge (appointed by Governor Richardson, former Ambassador to the United Nations, who was passed over by Barack Obama for the Vice President position, and who directed that "all State flags" be lowered to "half-mast"  for Cire's services) declared Cire to be dead on January 26, Cire's Birthday.

- **January 27** -- Cire's "digital communications" end on January 27.

Cire Grebgnuoy @EricYoungberg · 1h
Police noted his last text message of "fever" ... and took photos of his blackberry showing last message "I'm taken ill ..."

○ His last emails involving "Treasurer" discussions were made on the morning of January 27.

○ A nebulously apocryphal January 27 police report suggests Cire died that day, although for some reason lists the *year* of death as 2009, rather than 2010.

○ The last call from Cire's Blackberry (made to a Barr brother phone) was recorded on January 27, at the precise minute Barack Obama started his State of the Union speech that evening.

For all practical purposes, despite the conclusion from the conniving lawyers and dark probate Judge that Cire died on January 26, he is presumed to have been alive on January 27.

- **January 28** -- Cire's perversely political friends claimed he died on January 28. And that is what they wrote in his obituary. Months later

I was provided a dubious "official" death certificate. It states Cire died at 8:55 PM on January 28, 2010, with a possible cause of death being "internal bleeding."

Date	Time	Number	Rate	Usage Type	Origination	Destination	Min.	Airtime Charges	Long Dist Other Chg
1/24	11:43A	505-401-8540	Off-Peak	M2MAllow	Albuquerqu NM	Albuqurque NM	2	—	
1/24	12:19P	505-401-8540	Off-Peak	M2MAllow	Albuquerqu NM	Incoming CL	1	—	
1/24	12:20P	505-830-4110	Off-Peak	N&W	Albuquerqu NM	Albuqurque NM	1	—	
1/24	12:21P	505-401-8540	Off-Peak	M2MAllow	Albuquerqu NM	Albuqurque NM	1	—	
1/24	4:11P	505-401-8540	Off-Peak	M2MAllow	Albuquerqu NM	Incoming CL	2	—	
1/24	4:13P	505-401-8540	Off-Peak	M2MAllow	Albuquerqu NM	Albuqirque NM	4	—	
1/24	4:22P	505-453-7025	Off-Peak	N&W	Albuquerqu NM	Incoming CL	2	—	
1/24	4:27P	505-453-7025	Off-Peak	N&W	Albuquerqu NM	Incoming CL	2	—	
1/24	4:59P	505-301-1133	Off-Peak	M2MAllow	Albuquerqu NM	Incoming CL	4	—	
1/24	8:41P	505-401-8540	Off-Peak	M2MAllow	Albuquerqu NM	Albuqurque NM	1	—	
1/24	8:44P	505-401-8540	Off-Peak	M2MAllow	Albuquerqu NM	Incoming CL	3	—	
1/25	2:06P	505-864-7716	Peak	PlanAllow	Albuquerqu NM	Belen NM	2	—	
1/25	3:39P	505-239-0348	Peak	M2MAllow	Albuquerqu NM	Albuqurque NM	10	—	
1/25	4:50P	505-515-6030	Peak	PlanAllow	Albuquerqu NM	Albuqurque NM	2	—	
1/25	4:52P	000-000-0086	Peak	PlanAllow,CallVM	Albuquerqu NM	Voice Mail CL	3	—	
1/25	4:54P	505-222-4005	Peak	PlanAllow	Albuquerqu NM	Albuqurque NM	2	—	
1/25	5:30P	505-515-6030	Peak	PlanAllow	Albuquerqu NM	Incoming CL	1	—	
1/26	10:34A	505-268-6070	Peak	PlanAllow	Albuquerqu NM	Incoming CL	1	—	
1/26	12:19P	000-000-0086	Peak	PlanAllow,CallVM	Albuquerqu NM	Voice Mail CL	3	—	
1/26	12:54P	505-301-1133	Peak	M2MAllow	Albuquerqu NM	Incoming CL	1	—	
1/26	4:36P	505-577-0729	Peak	PlanAllow	Albuquerqu NM	Santa Fe NM	5	—	
1/26	4:41P	505-268-6070	Peak	PlanAllow,CallWait	Albuquerqu NM	Incoming CL	3	—	
1/26	7:24P	208-255-2748	Peak	PlanAllow	Albuquerqu NM	Incoming CL	5	—	
1/27	10:12A	505-268-6070	Peak	PlanAllow	Albuquerqu NM	Incoming CL	2	—	
1/27	10:34A	505-319-3199	Peak	PlanAllow	Albuquerqu NM	Incoming CL	3	—	
1/27	3:18P	505-280-1287	Peak	M2MAllow	Albuquerqu NM	Albuqurque NM	4	—	
1/27	7:06P	505-401-8540	Peak	M2MAllow	Albuquerqu NM	Albuqurque NM	4	—	

→Time of State of Union Speech

POLITICO

> TIME OF "LAST CALL" FROM CIRE's BLACKBERRY

Obama's state of the Union transcript 2010: Full text

01/27/2010 07:06 PM EST | Updated 02/05/2013 02:25 PM EST

Here is the transcript for President Barack Obama's first State of the Union address as delivered:

THE PRESIDENT: Madam Speaker, Vice President Biden, members of Congress, distinguished guests, and fellow Americans:

Our Constitution declares that from time to time, the President shall give to Congress information about the state of our union. For 220 years, our leaders have fulfilled this duty. They've done so during periods of prosperity and tranquility. And they've done so in the midst of war and depression; at moments of great strife and great struggle.

It's tempting to look back on these moments and assume that our progress was inevitable — that America was always destined to succeed. But when the Union was turned back at Bull Run, and the Allies first landed at Omaha Beach, victory was very much in doubt. When the market crashed on Black Tuesday, and civil rights marchers were beaten on Bloody Sunday, the future was anything but certain. These were the times that tested the courage of our convictions, and the strength of our union. And despite all our divisions and disagreements, our hesitations and our fears, America prevailed because we chose to move forward as one nation, as one people.

Again, we are tested. And again, we must answer history's call.

8

House Call

On the wintry evening of January 28, 2010 I was at my desk in my private study, across the yard from our house. In those days, being consumed with

work during the day and exploring Twitter at night (after family time had ended), I spent lots of time cloistered in my study.

While working I received a text from Cire's Blackberry. Cire (or, as it later occured to me, *possibly someone else* with Cire's Blackberry) asked that I "follow" the Speaker of the U.S. House of Representatives on Twitter. One click later I was following John Boehner (@SpeakerBoehner)[24]. Instantaneously afterwards I received an automatically generated tweet thanking me for the follow.

---

[24] John Boehner, speaker and majority leader of the House of Representatives, was responsible for authorizing funds for unconstitutional activities like (i) incarcerating people at GITMO, (ii) overseas wars, and (iii) surreptitiously monitoring and following private US citizens.

January 28, 2010

Speaker John Boehner @SpeakerBoehner   28 Jan 10 >
Thanks very much for the follow. Your input is important to me and
my colleagues in Congress. Please visit gopleader.gov for more
in

While reading the tweet and preparing to reply to Cire (or whoever had his
Blackberry) that "the follow" was successful, my Blackberry rang. It was my
wife calling from the house speaker phone.

Phone call with wife

Me: *Hey sweetness !*

Wife: *He's gone.*

Me: *Who's gone?*

Wife: *Cire. He's gone. He passed away during the State of the Union speech
last night. The police just found him ... dead ... [long pause ...]*

Texts with Cire's Blackberry

Me: Wife says you are dead.

Cire (or whoever was on Cire's Blackberry): Just go with it.

Phone call with wife

Me: *OK. I will be right in.*

It was difficult to know then what my wife and/or my brother (or whoever was on his Blackberry) were up to.

Was my brother really dead ? Or was this just another example of one of Cire's notoriously clever "life hacks?" Cire liked to do that.

PART II

Cire's Services

Where's the body?

-- Cire's interpretation of "habeas corpus"

9

Plane Ride
(to New Mexico)

The following day while flying to Cire's funeral alone (my coy wife explained she was going to fly down later with our kids), I had a chance to reflect on Cire's life and further debate with myself whether my cunning brother was actually dead or my secretive and increasingly evasive wife had just sided with my brother's political career over our very own family.

Complicating matters was that tension in our family had been strained since Cire last visited. My wife, enamoured with Cire's political successes, had inexplicably spent most of our first son's third birthday night (over the Thanksgiving holiday) alone with Cire at a cozy cabin down the road. And now with the recent birth of our second son, whose conception was tied up with the date of Cire's visit, she was the interest of the village. With Cire either now dead or faking his death (with my undercover wife's help), tension in our family was certain to increase.

Anyways, I processed Cire's "passing" into the following options:

1. **Cire is <u>not</u> dead.** The text from Cire's Blackberry on January 28 really was from Cire who was, and is, still alive. People are just faking Cire's death for political purposes. The report of Cire's death is just "fake news."

2. **Cire <u>is</u> dead.** If so, the text from Cire's Blackberry on January 28 must have been from someone else with Cire's Blackberry because the text was received *after* Cire was supposedly already dead on January 27, according to my wife.
   a. *Murdered.* Maybe Cire was brutally murdered. That is what my wife's twin sister suggested ("assassinated by the mafia" was one of her theories) and that did seem at least plausible presuming Cire was actually dead. Of course this was/is the same sister-in-law, a "family doctor," who once claimed to not want to comment on X-rays for my dad because of "fear over liability" while her husband the surgeon joked "he's toast" and has advocated for a new kind of tax, the "Dad Tax," ever since.
   b. *Suicide.* Maybe Cire killed himself. That is what my wife faintly suggested.
   c. *Natural causes.* Maybe he died from his "cold?"

From there I began to retrace my most recent communications with Cire. After connecting a few dots Cire's passing seemed likely tied to politics. I began recalling our last conversation that took place at his New America "White House" where Cire was just reported dead, and the topic of elections.

10

Elections

A primary conversation thread with Cire the last time we met was elections, and specifically Presidential elections. Cire was eager to share thoughts on their progression. He could persuasively argue that all Presidential elections since 1804, when the blatantly unconstitutional 12th Addendum was ratified but which had never passed muster with the Supreme Court, were unconstitutional and thus void. On the night of our last supper we reminisced on Presidential elections from 2000 to present.

- <u>2000 Election.</u> At the start of the new millennium, two candidates for President each received the most votes depending on which way the votes were counted. To resolve who the President was, the Supreme Court Chief Justice John Roberts determined the President to be the son of the father who, when serving as President, had appointed him Chief Justice. Cire always grinned when pointing out this election clustermess -- with errors of apparent conflicts of interest[25].

---

[25] Part of the reason that Jefferson established an elaborate Electoral System in the original Constitution for selecting the President was to avoid a very issue like this one

The following year 9/11 catastrophes were featured on lots of televisions. For many people who had ditched their televisions (either replacing them with the Internet or electing to go "off the grid") 9/11 was just another politically staged series of events in a long line of embellished war folklore -- one especially "made for television." It would be, perhaps, the last large-scale memorable television event before the Internet took over and changed the world.

The good news was that whether 9/11 was "real" or "real fake" the aftermath was helping New America. It was inspiring the notion of "world peace" and making a cleaner planet a reality as New America's clean electric vehicles replaced Old America's gas-guzzling fleets, notorious for polluting the skies, rain and rivers everywhere after consuming blood-stained barrels of fuel from overseas.

#ReadingMakesACountryGreat

Cire Grebgnuoy @EricYoungberg · 55m
Can you hear me now ...

#VerizonUp
#RespectTheConstitution
#VotingRiotsAct

From a domestic economic standpoint 9/11 was also helpful, especially to the regions west of the Mississippi River with oil -- like those on top of the Permian Basin (where President Bush's Ranch is located in Texas) and the Julesburg Basin (near where Vice President Cheney's Ranch is located in Wyoming). Notably both basins, along with America's other strategic oil reserves, are known to have sufficient oil to meet the continent's needs for hundreds of years, or more likely, until America successfully transitions its energy consumption from "fuels from hell[26]" to "fuels from heaven[27]". Long term it is unwise to continue to extract fuels from the earth that are known to harm the climate (and trash the planet). It is worse though, indeed reckless, to import them into America from across the ocean.

- <u>2004 Election.</u> We didn't talk much about this election. We just kinda acknowledged it. Again this was the election held on the day our father, a tax accountant known for promoting the idea of "working one's way out of a job" had died. Our sister had advised us both of his passing with phone calls, and followed the news by reciting her version of the lord's prayer.

---

[26] Fuel extracted from *beneath* the Earth's surface (like Oil and Coal), which are not sustainable, and the use of which are known to be adversely affecting the earth's climate.
[27] Fuel, or more accurately, "energy" harvested from *above* the Earth's surface (like Wind and Solar) which is sustainable (at least until the sun stops shining) and clean.

God bless our Father who art' in heaven, hallowed be thy name. Thy kingdom come. Thy will be done on earth as it is in heaven. Give us this day our daily bread, and forgive us our trespasses, as we forgive those who trespass against us, and lead us not into temptation, but deliver us from evil. For thine is the kingdom and the power, and the glory, forever and ever. Amen.

- <u>2008 Election</u>. In November of 2008 there was another disputed election. Barack Obama, a constitutional law professor navigating increasingly turbulent political waters, won by a landslide. Yet some were rightfully concerned about the constitutionality of the election process and even his eligibility to be President, especially with the slippery slope of a Kenyan from Hawaii, being half an ocean away, coming into play.

One argument was that someone born in Kenya or even Hawaii can't be President because they are not a "citizen born naturally of America" as contemplated by the founding fathers and summarized in the Constitution. The idea being that if a President was not born on the continent of America, his allegiances might be more towards wherever he was from, rather than the continental United States of America. For example, if a President was born in Britain or one of its colonies (like Kenya) it was entirely foreseeable and concerning that America might quickly be subsumed back into the portfolio of the Crown.

Cire added fuel to the fire, sharing what he had garnered from semi-private conversations in the Oval Office at the White House (the real one), that the government had long been involved in breeding experiments, including "test tube babies." By carefully "baking" an experiment in a womb for the requisite period of time, it was possible to create -- albeit unnaturally -- a new life form[28]. These military-grade weapons (essentially human bots) were ineligible to be President for the reason they are not "naturally born citizens."

The general consensus, or at least a popular one with "some" of Cire's friends, was that Barack Obama was not actually President. He simply couldn't be. He was ineligible, for one reason or another.

Sure, lots of "voters" celebrated that Barack was President. But, then again, many of these same people celebrate, with just as much vigor, Santa Claus. In any event the process for electing Barack was fundamentally flawed and

---

[28] Many "unnatural" life forms, popularly acknowledged and known about for centuries, involve new cross-breeds of cats, dogs, horses and other domesticated animals. Since the time of the drafting of the Constitution it has been suspected that one or more of our highly-competitive 'orphaned' founding fathers may have been the product of similar "unnatural" breeding. Hence, the constitutional provision that to be eligible to be President, one must be "naturally born," except for the Founders who were already then "Citizens of the United States."

unconstitutional, according to many. For these "doubters," the story of Barack being President was just another example of "fake news."

There were *lots* of explanations of "why" Barack could not actually be President. Most concluded by addressing the legitimacy of his sketchy birth certificate from Hawaii. While contemplating this I began wondering when, or if, an "official" death certificate would be issued for Cire and what would be listed as the cause of death. It then occurred to me that, for whatever reason, I had never seen a death certificate for our Dad who had passed away years earlier on election day.

11

Dad's Passing

In striving to mentally process Cire's passing I began to reflect on our Dad's passing.

The funeral services for our Dad were somber yet hopeful. No one had actually seen Dad dead. And our sister who had reported him "gone" had only heard about his departure from a Korean friend who had supposedly shared "last supper" with him yet whose conversations were often lost in translation.

Further, most of the stories at Dad's "roasting" being held at the University Championship Golf Course, where Dad had scored virtually impossible back-to-back "eagles" on 9/11, were about Dad's great sense of humor and how much he enjoyed golf.

Dad was well-known for his hilarious laugh and loved for a lifetime of achievements, including those on the golf course. A couple of his more famous feats involved the two finishing holes at the University Championship Course, which happened while two planes were shown on television punching holes in New York's World Trade Centers on 9/11.

The "seventeenth" hole is an almost unreachable 230-yard uphill par three into the wind. From all accounts Dad hammered his 1-iron and "swished" a hole-in-one simulataneously with a jet nailing the first World Trade Center.

Minutes later Dad teed off on the "eighteenth" using his lofted rescue club. From the middle of the fairway, about 150 yards out, he then "rolled in" a 7-iron for another "eagle" -- at the very same time a second jet was shown toppling into the adjacent World Trade Center.

Dad's funeral services were now being held at the same golf course where he hit these miraculous golf shots. On 9/11, University officials roared and howled as they rushed out of the clubhouse towards the eighteenth green to congratulate Dad on his ace (followed by another "eagle"!!!) and alert him to events unfolding back East. Now these same University officials were hosting Dad's memorial services.

After the services Cire and I met at his house and decompressed from the events of the previous few days. Dad was dead -- although it still seemed surreal. How could our otherwise healthy dad be gone at the early age of 63? It did not make sense. Anyways, a few days earlier, we had buried his coffin in the graveyard near an adobe family chapel where I was married the previous year, and today we had just done an extensive "meet and greet" with scores of Dad's friends and golfing buddies.

That afternoon I was going to drive solo[29] to our family "shack" in the mountains where my Mom and sister were staying. Cire was going to stay in town with his new girlfriend. Until then we had time for a tour of Cire's house renovations (his new girlfriend had painted a wall), a Coors (in honor of Dad of who believed "beer should be regional"), and a game of pool (a "Championship of the World") on granddad's vintage pool table.

The pool table, from the early 1900's was exceptionally nice yet had always played just a bit "slow," mostly due to its heavy wool felt. And, although it had been well taken care of, the table's brass nameplate was tarnished with almost a century of play. Those were the defining characteristics of an anotherwise mint condition antique pool table.

The table was in the living room of Cire's Old America "investment" house that he would later trade away to a golfing buddy for his New America "White House."

All of our major family life events, especially weddings and funerals, were punctuated with a match on the pool table. The "last" Championship of the World was played on that day, following Dad's memorial services. Cire racked. I broke and ran the table -- somewhat of a rarity for either of us on the old and slow table.

---

[29] My unfamily-like wife was insistent that I attend my Dad's funeral services without her. She didn't join me for his services, or for the burial of his coffin.

We shook hands and bid each other farewell. We didn't really ever talk much about Dad's passing after that. We just kinda acknowledged it.

So Dad was dead. And now Cire.

It was challenging to process all the possibilities of what was going on.

Gradually the plane descended over the Native American lakes where Cire and I used to fish with our grandfather, and we landed.

12

The Four Musketeers

New Mexico is where Cire and I grew up together and attended school. Mom still lives there in our childhood home. That is where I was greeted by the "Four Musketeers" -- a quartet of Cire's political friends wailing songs of Cire's passing.

- **Campaign Manager** -- Cire's campaign manager was director of the New Mexico Film office. He shared how he had helped clean up Cire's "blood-stained walls" earlier in the day. He then nonchalantly reported that he had found a couple of pairs of Dad's cowboy boots which had recently been "re-soled" in the den, kept one pair and given the other pair to the "Godfather."

- **The "Godfather"** -- This mutual family friend then mentioned he hid some files *burying* "westside" "no doc" "handshake" loans in the closet of the "White House" and that Cire's mortgage broker had claimed "Cire's safe with no docs." Sure enough he was wearing a pair of Dad's ageless ole boots.

- **"West" land agent** -- This opportunistic real estate guru was a friend from Cire and my soccer-playing days. He was mostly speechless yet would pipe in periodically about the "importance of family."

- **"Insurance broker"** -- This squalid joker, turned politician, whom I had never previously met or heard of, stayed for more than a full working shift, long past the time everyone else had left. He made sure I understood that everything, even Cire's long term umbrella policies, were properly *pre-funded*. Towards midnight the Cinderella party was over as he began to ramble on that he was actually a "special forces Somalia" mercenary for Cire, friends and family.

These were Cire's political associates.

13

Last Text

Cire's last text message of "I'm taken ill" -- sent on his birthday of January 26, 2010 right after we last spoke -- was hazily shown on a police photo of Cire's Blackberry.

Conflicting with this, however, was the puzzling police report noting Cire's last text message was "fever" sent on January 27, 2009. This was and remains a questionable discrepancy of messages and times (by a year and a day).

as Nyquil.

I examined Eric's cell phone, which was on a dresser adjacent to his bed. It appeared that the last text message that he sent was on 1/27/09 at 1652 hrs that said "fever".

Janet reported last speaking with Eric at approximately 1000 hrs, 1/26/09.

OMI personnel (D. Wasko) responded to the scene and processed it. He did not report observing anything suspicious at the scene or to Eric's body. Eric's body was later removed from the scene by Brookwood transport and taken to the OMI. I took additional images of Eric's body and the bed after Eric's body was moved for transport. Nothing of a readily apparent suspicious nature was noted.

I submitted one CD of my images into evidence for processing.

VIGIL, S   DET   2696

Although the date of Cire's death was strangely uncertain, it did seem plausible that Cire might have had a "fever." This was both consistent and inconsistent with what Cire had told me on his birthday of January 26 -- that he had a "cold." And with classic Cire ambiguity, there was a bottle of cough syrup for "colds and fevers" on his nightstand.

Celebration of Life Services and Funeral

The Celebration of Life Services and Funeral for Cire were held a few days later at a colossal cathedral where Cire and I once sang in the choir in our childhoods on Christmas morning. The church was enormous, and packed to the gills for Cire's services. The wings were full. The balconies were full. The aisles were full. It was already "standing room only" before busloads of Legislators arrived from the State Capitol at the Governor's direction.

In the front row (a place I generally try to avoid), with my morbid wife (who had flown in by herself that morning, deciding to leave our young sons at home with the neighbors[30]) on one side and my mother on the other, the stories began on how hilarious Cire was. The services ended with two New Mexico armed officials lowering an Old America "red, white and blue" flag in a dignified ceremony, folding it into a triangle, about the same size as a rack of pool balls, and handing it to my Mom as a souvenir.

---

[30] Perhaps it was just coincidence, yet more likely another indication of how deeply Cire had penetrated into our village, that one of the neighbors recently had starting dressing up as Santa for Christmas (on the anniversary of when God's son was born) and his wife loved being the Easter bunny (on the anniversary of when God's son "reappeared from the dead"). Both started playing their "roles" to the absolute delight of my wife, right after Cire's last visit to town.

A massive church overpopulated with mourners had just participated in services for Cire and I was increasingly convinced Cire's passing was politically motivated, and possibly just a hoax.

After the church services concluded there was a reception at the country club, just a short drive from the church and about a 9-iron from Cire's "White House."

The surreal stretch of limos carrying family, cousins and loads of Cire's friends arrived first. Some mutual friends, however, were already at the country club, having just finished a round of golf in the blustery winter wind rather than sit through the church skewering. Parties were choosing sides fast.

The first friend I talked with reaffirmed what was going on. The stakes were high. A brotherly war of biblical proportions had effectively just been escalated for at least another generation.

Waves of Cire's admirers paid respects. His harem of elegantly graceful highschool girlfriends expressed shock at Cire's sudden passing and surrounded me with smiles. My turbulent wife, draped in black, left early after throwing a sordid temper tantrum and flew back home despite the burial of Cire's coffin, at the family graveyard next to the church where we were married, being scheduled for the following day.

The burial of Cire's coffin was sparsely attended, which was surprising. My wife's not attending seemed odd, yet she insisted it was nothing more than wanting to get home to be with our sons. My sister's not attending seemed even more odd.

In any event, a few of us buried Cire's coffin in our snow-covered family graveyard. Lots of emotional feelings. Mom was convinced Cire was dead. She was overwrought with sadness, standing next to me crying.

The others, just a handful of distant family members, all from out of state, were placidly discussing how nicely their rental cars performed in the snow. Nobody had rented a Hertz® because everything about them, from their "bait and switch" agents to their vehicles, sucked. People continued reminding each other that the only thing good about a Hertz® was the commercial from years ago featuring OJ Simpson rushing through an airport on his way home to slice up dinner for his wife. These were all favorite conversation topics of Cire's.

Box of Bank Documents

The day after Cire's coffin was buried, Mom and I visited Cire's "White House" where he was declared dead. The Godfather had, for some unknown reason at the time, clandestinely hidden a "box of bank documents" in a closet of the den. The box contained lots of original documents for the New America "White House" and paperwork tied to several Old America recreational vehicle parks.

While we considered options for eventually wrapping up Cire's estate, there was a knock at the door.

Visit from Bank President

At the door of the "White House" was the dapperly cheerful president of a New Mexico bank (which Cire had helped establish in December of 1999 just before Y2K), who was a family friend. He had with him not flowers or words of condolences, but questionable paperwork regarding a non-performing loan that Cire was supposedly on the hook for. He also had a receipt for funds he swiped for/from Vasa for Cire based on a conversation at the country club.

As he was welcomed into the house the conversation continued. The bank president was kind enough to alert us that the bank's parent company in Dubuque, Iowa (located on the western bank of the Mississippi River) was going to try to bury lots of "westside" "no doc" 'handshake' loans on property with disputed title along with Cire. The loans at issue, he explained, had a scheduled value equal to "roughly the debt the U.S. owes China."

Then he provided me with the following documents.

- An illegible copy of an "unlimited guaranty" purportedly from Cire guaranteeing loans to a recreational vehicle park in Texas with disputed ownership. The RV park, which Cire was no longer a part of, was now being run by a client of the bank, one of the Barr brothers, who had traded the "White House" to Cire, where Cire was reported dead just days earlier and where we were now standing.

- An illegible copy of a debit/credit slip confirming that a boatload of cash had been transferred either to/from Vasa, a transfer which the bank president had evidently approved on a phone call.

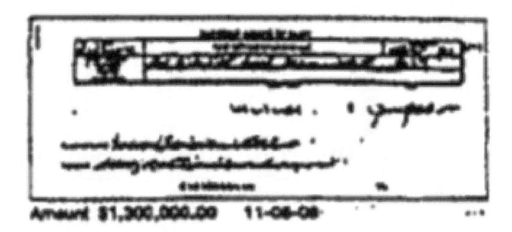

- Bank statements burying "weapons of mass financial destruction," including more than $100 billion in Alphabet Tranche (from A to Z) loans effectively consolidated in September of 2008 --- all tied directly to the US Government's Troubled Asset Relief Program (TARP).

Many of these loans were for properties on the border of the United States and Mexico, downstream from Cire's village that was notable for putting water back into the river that was cleaner than it removed -- a village with Intel®⁾ inside on Navajo land.

After delivering the paperwork the bank president mentioned that he had recently traded golf clubs with Cire (they were both left-handed) and how much he enjoyed golfing with Cire. After we bid farewell he walked across the street for lunch at the country club while Mom and I continued inventorying Cire's estate items.

We found Cire's laptop safely tucked away in a leather briefcase from my early law career. Cire had "swiped" the briefcase when I was traveling years earlier. Cire let me have it again when I returned. Then somehow Cire ended up with it. Since Cire was officially "dead" and I was being appointed Personal Representative of his estate, I was happy to have my briefcase back to work on his estate. I plugged in the laptop and let it charge.

Most of everything else was accounted for except Cire's passport. Never located that. This encouraged thoughts that maybe Cire was travelling, maybe on his ship, and not really dead.

The one item noticeably missing from the "White House" that I was anxious to review and that was supposed to be delivered to me soon was Cire's

Blackberry. At Cire's "Celebration of Life" services, right after my distempered wife left in a tizzy, the Godfather told me that he now had Cire's Blackberry.

17

Blackberry and Gmail

Moments after the bank president left there was another knock at the door. This time it was the Godfather (a mutual friend of Cire's and the bank president). After Cire passed away he had covertly hidden a box of questionable bank documents in a closet. Now, he had Cire's Blackberry and Gmail login credentials, and wanted to pass them along. Mom and I offered that he join us inside for a visit. He was getting ready to tee off with his afternoon group so he couldn't -- otherwise he would have. He just wanted to pass along the goods.

Receiving the login info for Cire's Gmail account was perplexing. Why did the Godfather have Cire's login credentials? Anyway, I was happy to now have them. Cire's Gmail account would hopefully help answer questions about his passing.

Reviewing Cire's Blackberry, more questions arose. The text message to me from January 28 (requesting that I follow the Speaker of the House of US Representatives on Twitter) had been purged. Who had deleted the text conversation? And why?

Anyway, I logged into Cire's Gmail account and that is when things got really weird, really fast. Prominently featured were two email threads, both of which discussed the legend of Cire possibly impregnating women who were married to someone else. One email thread was from a mutual friend. The other was from my wife.

Both threads suggested, presumingly jokingly, that the sons thus born may be the result of a "second coming of God." In the case of my wife's perplexing emails to Cire, she stated that she *loved* (a term of endearment she never used in our communications) their time together on his previous visit to town (nine months before our second son was born), and was sorry he wouldn't be coming for Christmas. She "fervently hoped" he would be coming again for Easter.

God, Cire. Jesus H. Christ.

18

Plane Ride
(From New Mexico)

Since the last spurious phone call from my wife, when she apathetically advised me that Cire was "gone" and then in a more rattled voice that he was "dead," I had been contemplating Cire's passing. I was uncertain if Cire was really dead when receiving that call, and my mind had raced with possibilities the entire time flying to New Mexico. Now on the flight home to Spokane, after days of talking with family and trusted friends, I was even more uncertain.

I had received "lots" of clues that Cire's passing was suspicious and possibly unreal. Yet I also had talked with countless friends of Cire expressing sorrow over his death. I was flying back to an awkward situation. My housemate wife supposedly believed Cire was dead, and had even been the first to break the news. I was increasingly doubtful, however, especially now understanding that she had been unfaithfully communicating, unbeknownst to me, with Cire about our second son and plans for Easter.

On the way to the airport I had stopped at Cire's "White House" and picked up my ole briefcase, loaded with his fully-charged laptop computer. Now, with our plane at cruising altitude heading towards Spokane, I fired it up and began to explore. I opened up Cire's Gmail account again, and tried to make sense of things.

Cire Grebgnuoy @EricYoungberg · 1h

To hack the Country ... very democracy itself ...

an email account would be needed ...
with Russian companies watching Korean counterparts ...

so one was established ... with volatile generation skipping
weapons of mass surveillance and destruction instructions
encrypted

Clicking around it was obvious this was indeed a Cire political account. It was hilarious. Cire's Gmail account read like the greatest story ever told.

It serpentinely wove together tales of -

- God (referenced in a joke about a golfer surviving a terrifying lightning storm by raising his 1-iron to the sky because "not even God can hit a 1-iron")
- The second coming of God's son (a story my wife was puckishly nurturing in "dark mode" with Cire)
- Countless entertaining threads of #FakeNews

On the financial side of things, throughout the account Cire's mortgage broker effectively mocked the Federal Government for giving banks "free money" like Santa Claus. He was particularly sharp with the increasingly irksome U.S. Treasury TARP fund folks handing out more than $80 million to Cire's bank (the one headquartered in Dubuque, Iowa).

2008 Santa Claus Email

From: <jbakhtiar@msgroup.us> Mortgage Broker Jim
(https://www.youtube.com/watch?v=qC5vlle8b9I) escaping Iran on
horseback sharing "Eric's safe with No Docs"
Date: Tue, 23 Dec 2008 14:36:05 -0700
To: <youngberg23@gmail.com>
Subject: SANTA CLAUS MAY SEEK FEDERAL BAILOUT

SANTA CLAUS MAY SEEK FEDERAL BAILOUT

Possible Taxpayer Rescue Sparks Unprecedented Disagreement

Santa May Not be Coming to Town

By Alex R. Dahl
December 23, 2008

The email account weaved these humorous discussions together with Cire's far-reaching political responsibilities. Everything was nice, tidy and amusing. As an example, a two-column spreadsheet included a prioritized list of State funded projects in one column, ranked according to campaign contributions received by lobbyists to date, in the next.

Cire's closing batch of emails on January 27 (the day *after* the shady lawyers and foul probate court had declared Cire dead) involved "Treasurer" discussions with a triumvirate of clever Westerners. The theme of the conversation was that the only expenses the United States Treasury was authorized to spend money on were those expenses that were actually "constitutional." Other expenses, those that conflicted with the spirit and intent of the Constitution, were unauthorized and any funds wrongly expended were subject to being "clawed back."

To the extent that Congress had directed the Treasury to spend money on things that were unconstitutional, that was an ever increasing problem for them. Although they might not be guilty of Treason for their actions (but they could be[31]), they likely would eventually be held responsible to reimburse the funds.

Along these lines a New America Treasury was established with a $14 Trillion roundUps *surplus*. This counter-balanced, on a "one to one" basis, the then $14 Trillion *deficit* the Old America Treasury had managed to "rack up" by engaging in unconstitutional activities (like incarcerating people at GITMO for free speech violations, engaging in goofy wars overseas, and

---

[31] The Constitution provides that "Treason against the United States, shall consist only in levying War against them, or in adhering to their Enemies, giving them Aid and Comfort" (emphasis added), which of course was exactly what was going on.

monitoring US citizens with expensive surveillance systems which violate the constitutionally implicit "right to privacy"). As Old America's dollar deficit increased, New America's roundUps surplus would become more valuable.

For example, if Old America's deficits increased by 50%, from $14 Trillion to $21 Trillion, the value of New America's roundUps would be similarly increased. No new roundUps would be issued (they are fixed at $14 Trillion), it would just cost 50% more in dollars to obtain them. As radical as it sounds, Cire and his friends were going to "put an end" to US Dollars being foolishly spent on unconstitutional activities, and maybe even the US Dollar itself.

JAN 26

TREASURY OF $14 TRILLION
ROUND-UPS is hereby ESTABLISHED

82

Cire's first email was from 2005, after he visited my village north of Spokane. His last email on January 27, 2010 was "confirmation of a Treasury swap."

The range of emails over the course of the account was expansive. Some of the emails that immediately caught my attention were those in reference to:

- My neighbor in the Blue House (discussed in chapter 26) from New York living on "Native American land."
- My wife's mother and father, who were so bitterly divorced they refused to even speak to each other at our wedding in 2003. Reciting this story always gave Cire great joy. He used to say "it would take an act of God to get them on the same team again."
- "Weapons of Mass Financial Destruction" that Cire's bank president friend had mentioned just days earlier at the "White House."
- Our grandfather's pool table, and specifically a new kind of italian felt which might "speed up play."

Cire had put a LOT of thought into setting up and managing his "hysterical" political email account.

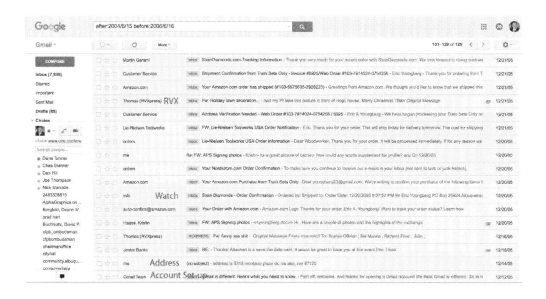

Increasingly it seemed that Cire's email account had been brashly populated with the intention of it serving, eventually, as the foundation for a hilarious movie of biblical proportions, complete with content from his friend and campaign manager, the Director of the NM Film Office.

Nick Maniatis, Director of NM Film Office

One email that received a bunch of attention was delivered on the day Cire was first reported dead. It addressed the question of whether Barack is a U.S. citizen, and thus eligible to be President. Simply enough the answer was "no" for the reason that even if Barack was really born in Hawaii (and not the

British colony of Kenya), Hawaii is not part of "America," the geographical limits of the United States as set forth in the Constitution.

Anyways lots to contemplate. I closed up Cire's laptop and prepared for landing. I was looking forward to being home, yet slightly anxious about what if anything more my wife had planned for me.

G☒ail
by Google

Cire Grebgnuoy <youngberg23@gmail.com>

---

lunch today; Fund;

Wed, Jan 27, 2010 at 5:32 AM

Democratic November Game Plan: Pray for GOP Suicide

Two respected political handicappers have grim news for Senate Democrats. Neither Larry Sabato of the University of Virginia or Nate Silver of FiveThirtyEight.com are anything close to GOP partisans. Yet both believe that if the midterm elections were held today, Democrats would lose seven seats even beyond their stunning loss of Ted Kennedy's seat in Massachusetts. They would wind up with 50 seats and the presumed support of independents Joe Lieberman and Bernie Sanders, leaving an emboldened GOP caucus of 48 members in a much stronger position to thwart President Obama's policies and appointments.

Robert Menendez, the New Jersey Democrat who chairs his party's Democratic Senatorial Campaign Committee, will issue a memo today launching his plan to minimize those losses. At its core his plan seeks to divide the Republican Party: "We have a finite window when Republicans candidates will feel susceptible to the extremists in their party. Given the urgent nature of this dynamic, we suggest an aggressive effort to get your opponents on the record."

Robert Menendez

The memo goes on to list a series of "gotcha" questions it urges Democrats to force their prospective GOP opponents to answer:

"Do you believe that Barack Obama is a U.S. citizen? Do you think the 10th Amendment bars Congress from issuing regulations like minimum health care coverage standards? Do you think programs like Social Security and Medicare represent socialism and should never have been created in the first place? Do you think President Obama is a socialist? Do you think America should return to a gold standard?"

Politico.com reports that the idea here is that "Tea Party" activists could be informed about any Republican who answers "no" to any of the questions, in hopes activists would "turn up the heat" and possibly force GOP candidates into embarrassing retreats in order to placate "extremist" elements in the GOP.

I'm dubious the strategy will work. While Republican Rep. Mark Kirk did retreat from his vote in favor of cap-and-trade climate legislation after he announced his candidacy for the U.S. Senate, Mr. Kirk's backtracking largely grew out of collapsing public support for fighting global warming rather than "Tea Party" pressure. If Massachusetts showed anything, both moderate Republicans and "Tea Party" activists were so scared of President Obama's agenda that they are likely to keep their internal divisions buried in the fall. "Obama lurched so far to the left that all the fire is being concentrated on him for now," says GOP pollster John McLaughlin. "I don't see Republicans forming a circular firing squad when they are enjoying watching Democrats have their own after Massachusetts."

Even some Democrats acknowledge that Mr. Menendez is simply putting out the best strategy he can under difficult circumstances. "He's got the worst hand to play of any DSCC chairman, ever," Democratic strategist Steve Murphy told Politico.com. "His job is to minimize losses in this economic environment. The notion that Democrats pick up seats or even hold what we have is not realistic."

— *John Fund*

Quote of the Day I

"They just kept telling us how good it was going to be. The president himself . . . said, 'Well, the big difference

86

PART III

Life in the Village
(After Cire's passing)

与朋友保持亲密关系，与敌人保持亲密关系

Keep your friends close, and your enemies closer

-- Sun-tzu, the Art of War

-19-

Condolences

After returning home several boorish neighbors visited again and again, over the course of the following weeks and months, at the request of my increasingly frenetic wife. Many, especially the neighbors who had recently started playing Santa Claus and the Easter Bunny, expressed repeated sorrow over Cire's passing. A few others chipped in for a memorial "family tree."[32] All around the village, Cire's passing (and his last visit when he spent most of the evening with my sly wife at a cabin down the road) were pervasive conversation topics for months and then years.

Those were taboo topics noticeably absent from our house. Never discussed. Not even once. For whatever reason my clammed-up wife was silent about Cire's passing and the night she spent occupied with him the last time he visited precisely nine months before our second son was born.

When I expressed doubts about Cire's passing to one neighbor couple, the wife insisted he must be dead. She then shared the story of her husband's brother who had just blown his head off with a shotgun on a macadamia nut

---

[32] Friends later planted the tree for Cire in a memorial zen rock garden near the village common area that a next-door neighbor was claiming by adverse possession.

plantation in Hawaii because of a US Bank loan he couldn't repay. She was certain Cire must have done the same thing or something similar. Her husband, a New York stock broker with Morgan Stanley who had survived 9/11 with the rest of his office at an off-site conference on Long Island that day, just complacently nodded before creatively masse-ing the conversation to Easter.

20

Pool Table Arrives
(Good Friday to Easter)

On the morning of Good Friday the pool table arrived. As I was out of town working on matters for Cire's estate, a few zealous villagers volunteered to set it up. They successfully accomplished the weighty task before I returned late that night. The following day, on Saturday, there was quite the party at our place with most of the village participating.

The husbands shot pool. The wives drank Bloody Mary's and busily prepared for a big Easter egg hunt scheduled for the following day. The kids and dogs played in the yard and welcomed the warm spring weather after a long winter of snow.

It was of course nice of the villagers to have set up the pool table. And it was generous of them to spend the day at our place, many consoling me, repeatedly, about how tragic Cire's passing seemed to be. Nevertheless, it was also slightly concerning with how excessively excited everyone was about Easter.

God's son has risen from the dead once before. Would that happen again …
and if so when? When and how would people learn of the second coming of
God's son? These were the questions asked, mostly by the garrulous tipsy
wives who, like my wife, claimed they *believed* that Cire was dead.

A few things were noticeably different about the pool table from the last time
I saw it at the 2004 Championship of the World. The name plate was shiny,
not tarnished, which could have been due just to the refinishing. And, the
table which always had played "slow" now played noticeably faster, perhaps
due to the new Italian cloth Cire had ordered for it -- which was referenced in
Cire's Gmail account. In any event, it was either the table we honed our skills
on growing up as kids, the "twin" pool table from the cantina or a very good
replica.

For the next few months, and then years, villagers played lots of games
(mostly "bank the eight") on the table and regularly noted that with it being
almost 100 years old, it had seen a lot of history. Indeed, the neighbors were
now confidently commenting, just as Cire had, that when the first games
were played on it there were no world wars, income taxes, or federal reserve
notes --- and women traditionally did not vote (although they certainly could
have with a very plain reading of the Constitution that provides "People"
shall choose their Representatives). A lot had changed in the last century.

Several villagers found and enthusiastically renovated similar vintage pool tables, which eventually resulted in the South Wooded Acres Pool Players Association ("SWAPPA") being formed with weekly league play. At these events neighbors would shoot pool, party, and consider options for exchanging (or "swapping") Old America for New America with villages, voting and taxes.

21

Tax Day

On Tax Day, April 15th, white-collared New Mexico bank officials formally disclosed that *two* loans had supposedly been made to an RV Park on Navajo Nation land which Cire had purportedly unconditionally guaranteed (which made Cire's estate liable for eventual repayment).

- Loan 036
- Loan 037

Later the loans were documented in a *New Mexico* Claim and *Texas* legal proceedings.

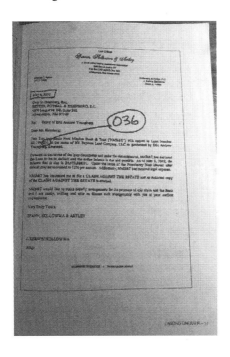
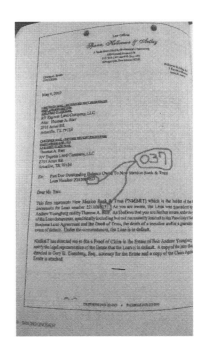

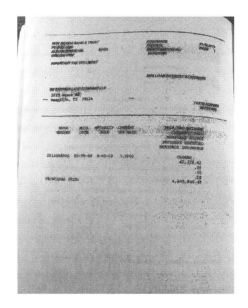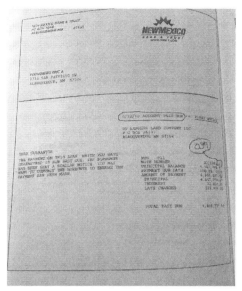

The suspicious paperwork seemed to be an attempt to bury, or maybe draw attention to, the actual *one* loan that indeed had been made, Loan 035, which was due for repayment the following year. Strangely, the Godfather had hidden copies of loan paperwork at issue, along with a bogus post-dated construction loan appraisal, in a closet of the "White House" while cleaning up after Cire's passing.

Details were sketchy. Transactions were increasingly questionable. There were now supposedly *three* loans in play on the same property which I understood from conversations with Cire actually only had *one* loan on it.

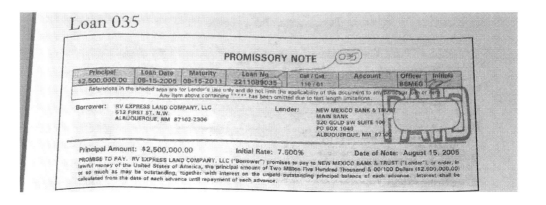

Loan 035

Soon after, the venerable New York Times published a comprehensive bank story on the Troubled Asset Relief Program (TARP), which was followed by the Small Business Loan Fund (SBLF). The story featured the Iowa bank concocting the Claim against Cire's estate and provided a quote from its Chief Financial Officer explaining "it's a bit of a [Navajo] shell game." Later the author, wearing a Navajo turquoise bead necklace, explained the basic version of the shell game (which involves one bead and three shells) in play with the three loans, two of which were hollow all the way, on prime time television.

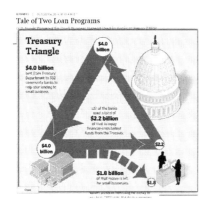

The stories of loans on Navajo Nation land, from lawyers, accountants and later the media, were increasingly hilarious, all making prolific fun of the irreconcilable nature of Loans 035, 036 and Loan 037.

In the end the rambling story went something like this. A seller from Brooklyn, on President Street, had sold Navajo Nation land (with open-ended borders essentially covering the entire continent of America) to a strawman for beads and cash to boot. Later, Cire sold the same land back to the Navajos, and used the proceeds to pay off (i) "one of the three loans" (it was never clear which loan one was repaid) at issue, AND (ii) a mortgage on a "no doc" construction loan wrapped up in an Old America like-kind Treasury Exchange which resulted in Cire obtaining his New America "White House." The bottom line, at least to Cire's title company, was that the Native Americans, and specifically, the Navajo Tribe, once again owned Brooklyn, Manhattan and everything else in America, *including the land upon which the White House was situated*, just like before the colonists settled in America.

That part was simple. The complicated part was the taxes. The overlapping and intertwined federal and multi-state income taxes layered on the transactions continued to increase in complexity until literally, no one, not even the Old America Treasury agents, could understand them.

This was perhaps the best indicator yet that Cire was likely still alive and harmonizing things. Taxes were a considerable part of our family history[33], and of particular interest to Cire. Cire was a firm believer that "taxes should be Constitutional" just like our founding fathers intended.

When establishing the Constitution the founders considered taxes carefully. After years of debate they resolved that the Federal government would tax the States, not the people. The precise language of the Constitution is here.

Taxes shall be apportioned among the several States

Nobody likes to pay taxes -- not even states. By mandating that "Taxes shall be apportioned among the several States [which "opt in" to the United States]" the Constitution protects against the Federal Government becoming an unsustainable industrial militarized "taxing machine" which taxes unreasonably

---

[33] Our grandfather, after retiring from the FBI, was a tax accountant. Our dad, following in his dads' footsteps, was a tax accountant. And our sister, with an advanced degree from the London School of Economics, and working for a global finance firm in Australia, was a tax accountant.

and excessively. The States effectively keep the Federal Government, and taxes, in check.

There are lots of good reasons for apportioning taxes among the States. There are perhaps even more good reasons to not tax individuals, business, trusts, estates and virtually anything else (no matter where situated) except for the States. To put it bluntly the 16th Amendment is absurd.

"ARTICLE XVI. The Congress shall have power to lay and collect taxes on incomes, from whatever source derived, without apportionment among the several States, and without regard to any census or enumeration."

In Cire's view, the change in the constitutional tax provisions *from* "apportioned among the several States" *to* "without apportionment among the several States" is one of the reasons Old America was broke, destined to collapse and would eventually start over with a clean slate, just like Thomas Jefferson suggested.

It was Cire's opinion that the Federal Government should not tax people individually. He was convinced that during his lifetime or maybe soon after he passed away, people would reach the same conclusion. Tax day had always been an enormously stressful day for our family of tax accountants. Cire was determined to bury it.

22

The Claim

On May 6, 2010, a New Mexico bank filed an "official" Claim against Cire's estate for an amount significantly in excess of the value of Cire's estate. Attached to the Claim were stacks of illegible bank documents from the bank's parent bank in Dubuque, Iowa, known for (i) its highly sophisticated digital imaging facility and (ii) having received over $80 million in TARP funds on the condition that its banks not engage in risky banking practices. On top of the copy of the Claim delivered to Cire's estate was a handwritten note, complete with a hashtag and smiley face.

> *If the government won't follow its own rules*
> *why have them in the first place?*
>
> *#AbolishTheFederalReserve :)*

The Claim was seeking to have Cire's estate repay the loans the bank had supposedly made to the Barr Brothers' RV Park business, based on a personal guarantee Cire had purportedly signed. It had several questionable features that made the Claim seem like a well-scripted prank.

- The Guarantee at issue had a signature that did not look like Cire's --- it was waaaay too <u>long</u>.

- The Promissory Note at issue had a signature that also did not look like Cire's for the opposite reason --- it was much too <u>short</u>.

- The Deed of Trust at issue had purportedly been notarized on a <u>Sunday</u>. And rather than being notarized at a title company or bank, it had been notarized by Cire's secretary at his new "White House."

Further, the Claim referenced "Westside" "No Doc" "Handshake" Mortgage Loans consolidated on September 30, 2008, all of which Cire had purportedly guaranteed personally, with an earth-shaking scheduled payment due of $100 Billion ("10% of Trillion"). This amount was about equal to the government's entire Fannie Mae and Freddie Mac housing loan portfolio at the time. The irony was thick as these "no doc" loans were consolidated at the very time TARP was enacted to protect the financial system from the crisis created by these very types of loans.

Finally, the Claim had lots of illegible loan digits burying previous banking concerns. Perhaps coincidentally, yet seemingly more likely not, the technique used for "pixelating" the images at issue was the precise technique Cire's notary had been taught years ago during some advanced

training. The Claim definitely looked like an inside job, possibly with Cire's secretary and perhaps even Cire, involved.

The Claim was finely crafted and had lots of red flags. It seemed like a further, and perhaps final, attempt to make a mockery of Old America's Treasury handing out free cash (now digitally !) to banks. Accordingly, it also seemed likely that Cire was indeed still alive and probably helping one bank or another "book" and "swap" its reserves from Old America dollars to New America roundUps.

12/19/2008	Heartland Financial USA, Inc.	Dubuque	Iowa	$81,698,000
12/19/2008	Intermountain Community Bancorp	Sandpoint	Idaho	$27,000,000
12/19/2008	Wintrust Financial Corporation	Lake Forest	Ill.	$250,000,000

Financial historians familiar with "triple witching options" will note the Claim effectively detonated cascading weapons of mass financial destruction around the globe. Moments after the Claim was filed, a breathtaking Flash Crash occurred in the U.S. domestic stock markets eliminating $1 Trillion of value (equivalent to TARP program itself) as institutional investors across oceans reverberated from the terrific cataclysmic shock.

In any event, despite the Claim initially seeming to be a "well-scripted prank," or perhaps more accurately a "nicely orchestrated punk," it really had been filed in the New Mexico courts and thus needed to be dealt with.

I met with a friend, a law school classmate from Spain (now dead) with an advanced tax degree from New York who could be trusted in challenging times. When a gang of Mexicans from the medical school had sliced all the Gringos' tires early on the morning of law school finals, he was there to give me a ride ... almost like he knew :)

He reviewed the funky bank paperwork and advised "deny the New Mexico Claim." This was consistent with what we had been taught in law school, and what the Navajos and Spanish had been striving for since New Mexico first made its Claim to statehood more than 100 years ago. And that is what Cire's estate did. Soon after, striving to avoid World War III, Cire's estate was headed to Mediation.

23

Mediation

For purposes of resolving the Claim, parties scheduled mediation in New Mexico. The titanic bank was gluttonously intent on devouring Cire's entire estate. Cire's estate wanted to sink the "too big to fail" bank to the depths of hell. Perhaps parties could resolve this increasingly volatile nuclear matter agreeing to split things down the middle.

Prior to attending mediation a neighbor, the New York stock broker who had survived 9/11 by attending an offsite conference in Long Island with his colleagues on that day of tragedy, coached me in preparation in my village near Spokane. He offered that the mediator would likely be a retired judge who made significantly more money now mediating for banks than he had working as a Judge. Next he reasoned that, as a consequence, the mediator was not going to be independent or impartial. Lastly he explained that the bankers were essentially clients of the Mediator and "guessed" that they all were probably golfing buddies.

I arrived at mediation and was greeted by the left-handed bank president who had given me the questionable paperwork on the day after Cire's coffin was buried. This was the same banker who Cire had traded golf clubs with before Christmas. The banker then introduced me to the mediator who, almost incredibly, was the retired judge with Dad's golf clubs !

As mediation teed off, the retired judge shared some hilarious stories about golfing at the country club. He also joked that he was "stunned with disbelief" about everything that had happened on 9/11 (it was unclear if he was referring to the planes asynchronously crashing into the World Trade Centers as a result of commands from a former CIA operative working from a cave in Afghanistan, or Dad's back-to-back "eagles" on the golf course). Lastly, he conceded that, despite best efforts, he was still unable to successfully hit the sweet spot with Dad's ole 1-iron.

After a day-long round of mediation, the retired judge suggested, and the bank president stiffly nodded in approval, that Cire's estate should consider options for settling the Claim and everything else with a "global agreement."

24

Global Agreement

After a few years of charged negotiations and considering all kinds of options, Cire's estate ended up resolving the Claim with a *Global Agreement and Release of Claims from the Beginning of Time (The "Global Agreement")*.

The Global Agreement was comprehensive. It covered lots of land in America, several parcels in Europe and even one region in Asia on both sides of the Great Wall. All of the property as issue, in one way or another, had been collateralized (oftentimes with "no doc" loans), wrapped up in the world-wide financial collapse of 2008 and aggregated into one massive $100+ Billion consolidated debt obligation, that Cire had purportedly personally guaranteed.

The Global Agreement was broadly consented to, with armies of lawyers having participated in its drafting . It was signed by almost countless parties who previously had "no doc" loans for their houses, representatives from the largest banks, Native American tribal leaders and State judges from where "most" of the land at issue was situated.

The Global Agreement was also, however, limited in scope. Although its "release of claims" covered every type of claim imaginable (including, but not limited to all claims to, or relating directly or indirectly to land, and all statutory claims[34]) it only applied retroactively, from the date of the Global Agreement to "the beginning of time."

Thus, any breaches of the Global Agreement, happening *after* the signing of the agreement would trigger new claims which could be pursued, and which needed to be "cured" to the extent possible, under the traditional common law of contracts.

The Global Agreement included the following provisions, all of which the bank breached.

- **Old Loan Documents**. The bank would provide actual, signed, "real" documents for the old loans at issue. *The bank refused saying there*

---

[34] This was a subtle, yet paramount, clause added by one lawyer who had recently been appointed to be an appellate state judge. She felt strongly that the courts, not legislatures, should make law. Legislatures, she believed, were best suited to creating agencies to build infrastructure for the public good, not restricting people's freedom or land with laws. Consequently, she added this profound clause which effectively made Common Law (Contracts, Property and Tort) with thousands of years of precedence the absolute law of the land at issue, rather than statutes more recently codified by legislatures. With that one clause she effectively made hundreds of years of codified law null and void, at least in the states participating in, and bound by, the Global Agreement

weren't any such documents because all the deals had been done with a handshake or via Cire's Blackberry.

- **New Loan**. The bank would provide Cire's estate funds tied to a new loan. *The bank refused explaining this was a "no cash" loan.*

- **War Memorial Soccer Fields**. Cire had dedicated a portion of a recent real estate development for a "war memorial"[35] soccer field on the west side of a new hospital and incentivized other communities to follow his lead. His friends were now intent on completing the soccer field in Cire's honor. The bank was insistent upon receiving the land reserved for the soccer field as part of the Global Agreement. As a concession to make the deal work Cire's estate "kicked in" the land with the condition that the bank would provide Cire's estate the "right of first refusal" to buy the land back. *Later the bank sold the land without offering it to Cire's estate. This spawned several media productions in communities interested in advancing Cire's idea of "play soccer rather than war".*

---

[35] Rather than have hospital doctors continually attend to the wounded with limbs missing from overseas wars, Cire envisioned them attending their children's soccer games on weekends and shaking hands with the opposition at the conclusion of each "battle" with congratulatory words on "a game well played." Cire wanted to replace the world's wars with the world's sport.

- **"White House" (and remaining US property).** Cire's estate would (i) sell the "White House" (and apply the proceeds towards legal fees escalating in a skirmish that the bank and Cire's Estate were now, almost unimaginably just a few years earlier, on the same side of) and (ii) transfer Cire's remaining US property, including the hacienda in the middle of the apple orchard, to the bank on the conditions that (a) Cire's agent (whose broker was wrapped up in a Ponzi scheme with the big house) could live there on a long-term lease, and (b) the bank would offer Cire' estate the right to buy back the sprawling house before selling it to anyone else. *Soon after, the bank locked Cire's agent out of the house and demolished it, leaving Cire's agent homeless.*

Included with the Global Agreement was an **Allonge (from France)** tied to the **The Louisiana Purchase**. One of the most contentious parts of negotiating the Global Agreement, and enforcing it afterwards, involved collateralized "underwater" mortgages on property at issue in fifteen states west of the Mississippi River -- all the property included with the Louisiana Purchase of 1803.

The Native Americans at the negotiating table had reminded everyone how ludicrous, and wrongful, it was for the United States to have "claimed" purchasing their land from France. The land never belonged to French. Thus, France had no right to sell it.

For these "First Americans" (e.g., Navajos, Apaches and Commanches), the notion that the United States could have purchased much of middle America from an Emperor in France who didn't have any rights to the land was, and remains, simply absurd.

The Louisiana Purchase had been ratified, yet wrongly[36] so, by the US Senate and then reluctantly consented to by Jefferson[37]. Soon afterwards, white

---

[36] The French could not sell land it did not have the right to sell and, consequently, thc US could not purchase the land from them, despite the Senate ratifying the "deal."

[37] Jefferson was concerned about the implications of the purchase, both short and long term. He predicted presciently that *"this little event, of France*

men carrying "guns and a piece of paper" would ride their horses into Indian camps and tell everyone to leave since the white men now owned the land. They would show a piece of paper documenting the purchase to the Native Americans who were unable to read it, much less understand it as the idea of "owning land" was a foreign concept to them at the time. If the "red skins" refused to leave immediately, the "white skins" would raise their guns[38].

After more than two centuries of being displaced, the Native Americans were now up to speed on the notion of property ownership. They were insistent on, and indeed enthusiastic about, having their ancestral land returned to them, especially since the Global Agreement was explicitly releasing "all claims from the beginning of time."

It took months but finally everyone involved -- including Judges from Spain, the country which originally "claimed" the Louisiana Purchase land before transferring it to France, enabling it to be later "sold" to the US -- agreed that the Global Agreement's "release of claims" applied to all lands of the Louisiana Purchase and other lands at issue. The only catch was that as a practical matter the repossession by Native Americans of some land in

---

possessing herself of Louisiana, ... is the embryo of a tornado which will burst on the countries on both shores of the Atlantic..."

[38] Usually the Native Americans were "outgunned." Their bows and arrows, tomahawks and spears, were unable to successfully compete with invaders's firearms. On a few occasions, however, the Native Americans were also armed with guns. In the end, whoever had the bigger guns generally won the argument, and the land.

Canada and three states included in the Louisiana Purchase yet not represented in the Global Agreement (i.e., Minnesota, Montana and North Dakota) could not happen immediately for the reason that in places like downtown Minneapolis, Minnesota (a former Native American campsite where US Bank was now headquartered), all hell would break loose with an immediate transfer without advance notice. To secure the lands that would eventually be rightfully restored to the "redskins" after the "whiteskins" had been notified and properly evicted (with force and scalped if necessary), an Allonge was granted to Cire's estate on behalf of all Native Americans.

When it was all said and done, the Global Agreement had achieved the virtually impossible. It had established consensus among parties on lands of the Louisiana Purchase and other lands at issue to start over with a "clean slate" -- just the Original Constitution.

Of course, not everyone was immediately convinced that the Global Agreement applied to them. Similar to the Native Americans hundreds of years ago discussing the Louisiana Purchase, some doubted it had ever really happened and, even if it had, did not believe it should apply to them.

For these skeptics, these conspiracy theorists, the idea that the Global Agreement would enable, and was actually requiring, much of the world to start over with a "blank slate" was simply "fake news."

25

Fake News

Fakes News, or at least debatable news, has been around since the earliest of communications. When Moses returned from the mountains, chisel and slate in hand, he broadcast to anyone willing to listen that God had given him the holy Ten Commandments. People debated then, just as today, whether this was real or fake news[39].

For thousands of years fake news, and debates over the accuracy of accounts, has been rampant. When Jesus was reportedly crucified at the cross until death, buried for days, and then somehow returned to life on Easter, people debated whether or not he was actually ever dead. Further they debated then, just as today, whether he was really God's son.

In more recent history, and in particular the twenty years of Cire's Master Plan from 2000 to 2020, there have been countless questionable news events,

---

[39] Further, the Commandments themselves generated a fair amount of controversy, which still has not been resolved. As one example, God purportedly advised that "thou shall not kill." Does that commandment forbid people from killing only other humans, or actually any of God's creatures like pigs, cows, birds and lambs? Ask s Jewish vegan and a Christian carnivore that same question, and you just might trigger a holy war over supper.

many of which have included deaths, which are simply unbelievable. A few examples are provided below which have generated enormous amounts of controversy.

New York (9/11)

The highest television ratings ever, with more people watching TV than at any other time in history, were recorded on September 11, 2001.

Every generation has their defining moment of history, an event so profound that people of the age can immediately recall where they were and what they were doing when they learned of the news.

For my grandparents it was Armistice day (the end of the first World War), broadcast via radio. For my parents it was the assiniation of John F. Kennedy, shared across America on black and white television. For my generation it was 9/11, broadcast to the world in color.

For me, 9/11 has always been questionable. Certainly 9/11 was carefully planned and well executed. It has, and remains, just a bit uncertain though as to who was actually involved in plotting everything. Was Osama Bin Laden (noted for being a former CIA operative living in a Afghanistan cave) really the mastermind? Or were things "queued up" a little closer to home?

On the morning of September 11, 2001 I was at our family shack, a modest cabin on my grandfather's ranch in the Manzano Mountains of New Mexico, preparing for a day of solo mindfulness meditation. A few years earlier, on a trip around the world, I had been introduced to Vipassana meditation in Kathmandu, and committed to the practice of mindfulness. Upon returning to America I built a small adobe mediation chapel secluded in the forested part of the ranch with the hope of being able to periodically retreat there for enlightening meditation.

The last time I had visited the shack, and rustic chapel, was New Years Eve of 2000 (Y2K). That night was a disappointment. I had invited a few people expressing interest to meditate at the chapel until midnight and maintain serene silence at the shack afterwards. My brother had invited a few friends to the cabin to play poker and drink whiskey until sunrise. The two groups did not mix well.

Anyways, not having experienced much peace on Y2K trying to synthesize two irreconcilable groups, I was looking forward to meditating on September 11, without any distractions. Just as I was about to leave the shack and start hiking to the chapel, the telephone rang. It was an old rotary phone, without "caller ID". Somewhat hesitantly, as I really did not want to be bothered with whoever was now calling, I answered.

Me: Hello ?

Caller: YOU ARE NOT GOING TO BELIEVE THIS. IT'S INCREDIBLE!

It sounded like a direct order. Something from the military. And it was being issued by a DARPA[40] Air Force guy proud of his training in "irreality" and "fake news" -- one those who had coincidentally spent the night at the shack on Y2K with his partner, also from the Air Force.

Well I was distracted -- again. He explained a long and complicated story about how a bunch of Saudi Arabians (whom had supposedly learned how to fly planes but not land them) had just hijacked a bunch of jets on the East Coast (from near where he studied at the Air Force) and were in the process of flying these volatile "missiles full of people" into predetermined targets, including BOTH of the World Trade Center towers, which would soon be imploding. He then, knowing that the shack does not have a television, asked me to go watch television and "see how unbelievable the events were."

Not quite sure what to make of it all, and stunned that my meditation practice had once again been interrupted, I somewhat grudgingly drove a few miles down the gravel road to my reclusive uncle's place. My

---

[40] The Defense Advanced Research Projects Agency is an agency of the United States Department of Defense responsible for the development of emerging technologies for use by the military including robots, "chipped canines" and engineered beings tasked with propagating propaganda.

anti-establishment hippy "almost off the grid" uncle had recently been elected as mayor for his rural town. Afterwards, to keep current on regional events, he traded some of his hand-crafted pottery for a used television set with a large "rabbit ears" antenna which was able to pick up public television broadcasts when weather conditions were just right, which they were on 9/11.

When I arrived, I told him about the report I had just received that was supposedly "unbelievable" and asked if we could turn on his television. We fired up his dusty old television and sure enough, just a few minutes later, a "special broadcast" started reeling that showed a plane crashing high into a World Trade Center. A few minutes later another plane was shown colliding into the adjacent World Trade Center, after which both buildings imploded --- just as described on the call.

Did the buildings really collapse? Yes.

Did people really die, or get injured? I simply don't know.

Sure, television, and later newspapers, reported that people died and were injured. But later, people who had supposedly died or were injured in the events introduced themselves and snickered that they were actually alive and perfectly healthy!

One person who reportedly had died, along with countless colleagues, worked for Morgan Stanley on the top floors of the World Trade Centers. He was the guy who coached me for mediation, and accurately anticipated that the mediator would be golfing buddies with the bankers. He and his co-workers had watched the events of 9/11 on television from their "off-site" conference on Long Island that day with as much disbelief as everyone else. His wife was the one who told me that I should believe, or at least pretend to believe, Cire was dead despite all the evidence to the contrary.

Another person wrapped up with 9/11 was my neighbor, a retired New York City police officer living in the Blue House (discussed in the next chapter) who had supposedly been critically injured during the aftermath of 9/11. He not only verbally confirmed 9/11 was a "staged media production" on several occasions, he had a pre-production video to prove it.

According to my neighbor who was the most vocal about 9/11 of anybody I have ever met, there were at least two "official" versions of what happened on 9/11. One portrayed the events as a shocking terrorist attack coordinated by a former CIA operative from a cave in Afghanistan. The other documented the entire media production as a very tightly planned "inside job" carried out by the unconstitutional Air Force[41]. Both it now seems, were possibly true.

---

[41]The brightest stars in today's Air Force understand that it is unconstitutional. Speaking in "Navajo tongue" these modern day "code talkers" are able to persuasively explain why the budget-breaking

The "legend" of his being critically injured in 9/11 though, as he proudly boasted, was just "fake news."

Boston (Marathon)

Boston is famous for a few things. For more than two centuries it has been held in great esteem for its "Boston Tea Party[42]." Boston is also revered for its annual Marathon, the most popular long-distance running race in the world. And, finally, Boston is held in the highest regard for its region's civilized stance on capital punishment -- there is none.

On the morning of April 15, 2003 (unconstitutional "Tax Day") which also happened to be Patriots Day (an annual holiday commemorating the first

conflict-causing Air Force should be "rolled into the Navy" (like the Japanese did with their Air Force at Pearl Harbor) to help facilitate the end of overseas conflicts. "Flying machines" have been contemplated for centuries and indeed the first successful hot air balloon flight was in the early 1700's. If the Founding Fathers had wanted America to have an Air Force, they would have included it in the Constitution. They didn't, for good reason.

[42] This barrel-heaving event was responsible for the fundamental tax provision in the United States Constitution requiring that the government tax the States, not the people. The Boston Tea Party established that there shall be "no tax without representation." This principle was codified by establishing the taxes shall be apportioned among the several States, and that States shall have representative governments.

battles of the American Revolutionary War) explosions at the Boston Marathon put all three notorities into play.

Two brothers of the opinion that the wars in Afghanistan and Iraq should be be ended (a popular line of thinking at the time, especially with those missing limbs from those wars, and a philosophy consistent with the very platform that Barack Obama, the then President of the United States had been elected upon), supposedly triggered two loud "booms" near the marathon finish line to make their case. Despite there being countless security cameras in the area and hoards of spectators broadcasting the race's finish on their smartphone cameras, *not a single camera captured the details of the explosions.* This is and of itself is incredible. Like unbelievable. Like NOT believable.

Over the course of the day news broadcasts reported that authorities were searching for the two brothers who had purportedly triggered the loud booms by exploding "german-engineered Bosch® pressure cookers" hidden inside black backpacks. The initial news accounts were difficult to believe and as more information was released the story became increasingly far-fetched.

Questionable footage showed people missing limbs but it was unclear if the pressure cookers had truly cost them an "arm and leg." Increasingly it seemed likey that these "handicapped patriots" had actually lost their limbs while fighting in wars, funded with their very own tax dollars, in Afghanistan and Iraq.

At exactly midnight my nextdoor neighbor, the retired New York detective complicit in the fake news of 9/11 living in the Blue House (discussed in the next chapter), called me while I was working in my study. He apologized for calling so late, but said he could see that my lights were on, so he knew I was awake. He then said, "YOU ARE NOT GOING TO BELIEVE THIS ... IT'S INCREDIBLE!"

He then emailed me a link to a news broadcast on the Internet that showed the Boston Police had captured the older brother. He was handcuffed and lying face down in the middle of an intersection, surrounded by police and police cars. We discussed whether this suspect, obviously now "in custody," needed to be advised of his Miranda rights[43]. On this we disagreed, but reached consensus that the older brother had from all appearances indeed been safely captured. When then bid each other goodnight.

The following day I read conflicting accounts of the events in the newspapers, and on the Internet. Rather than being safely captured, the older brother had supposedly been run over by a car driven by his younger

---

[43] Miranda rights are a set of instructions that are required, by the 5th Addendum to the US Constitution, to be given to a person taken into custody on suspicion of having committed a criminal act, before he can be questioned by police.

brother and was now dead. This news was inconsistent with the news I had seen the night before. I really don't know to this day which account of the events is accurate, or even if either is.

In any event, the younger brother was supposedly later apprehended and, despite Boston's governing state law which prohibits capital punishment, sentenced to death by the federal government. The Boston Marathon events, the fate of the older brother and the death sentence of the younger brother are effectively a perfect storm mixing media and politics. It remains unclear how much of the supposed Boston Marathon bombing was/is "fake news."

Perhaps the entire event was staged to simply trigger discussions on whether controversial subjects, things like death and taxes, are truly certain.

Fake Local News

Fake news, or at least debatable news, is often exaggerated at the local level and then amplified as it resonates back and forth from village to village. This was true of the "shot heard round the world" more than 200 years ago (nobody actually heard the shot except for those within listening range) as well as the "round the world shot" described below.

Before Cire passed away he had arranged for the establishment of several "war memorial" soccer fields in villages in the western half of America (everything "westside" side of the Mississippi River). All of the agreements were verbal -- "no docs" just "handshakes." The determination of which villages were to be provided funds for soccer fields was to be based on which ones could create the most buzz, the most interest in their communities, in having the next generation of athletes play the world's sport on fields of freshly-cut grass.

Villages competed in good nature, with legendary stories being embellished and repeated as far as reasonable. Rival villages then debated what part of reports were real, and what were exaggerated, or faked. Afterwards sparring villages tried to "top" the stories with even more unbelievable tales of their own.

An example of the ratcheting up of local stories follows:

On a beautifully crisp Saturday morning in a small mountain village, two youth soccer teams faced off on a rough dirt "westside" vacant lot serving as the local soccer field next to the railroad tracks. The coaches, with hopes of better fields for all their players in the future, improvised a soccer game that remains a local legend.

One coach's son, playing goalie, performed a difficult "round the world shot" which landed in his own goal. The fans went crazy -- and parents started dropping "F-bombs." Things escalated until the chief of police ended up separating the two coaches, one of which left the field after receiving a red card, "handshake" and "no doc" fine.

The story was good. It created lots of excitement in the community noted for its steadily increasing interest in better soccer fields. As a finale to the fireworks, one parent at the game called some friends at another soccer game being played at a park on the "eastside" of the Spokane tribe's land (at the headwaters of the Spokane River[44]) and said "YOU ARE NOT GOING TO BELIEVE THIS … IT'S INCREDIBLE! We just had, and finished, World War III !"

Soon after, villages tried to top the story with even more ridiculously preposterous hyperboles.

One news report featured local law enforcement officers assassinating a pregnant Native American at a "westside" emergency room as she was going into labor, killing both her and her baby. There were "no docs" at the hospital, just lots of "handshakes."

---

[44] The Spokane River is known for having "water clean enough to drink," at least historically. About 100 years ago settlers "confiscated" the lake where the river starts and completely trashed it. Today people in the lake community, and those downstream, are known for purchasing water in plastic bottles from China.

Of course, the Native Americans didn't take kindly to being mocked in what became known as the "Abortion by Cop" video. So, they retaliated with a video of their own, entitled "Cop assisted Suicide."

In this hilarious news broadcast, a chubby cop named Sgt. Moore was out moonlighting when he gave his gun to a guy on a "handshake" deal then took one to the chin for the team. He reportedly died on the "westside" of town, with "no docs" around.

All the above stories seemed, and still seem, incredible (like "not believable"), at least to a degree. At a minimum, news reports seemed to have mis-reported and exaggerated information. Nothing, however, with any of the above stories was as completely impossible to believe as what followed.

Soon after the story of Sgt. Moore spread across the land, I had taken my sons to the Oregon Coast for our family vacation. My distancing wife had elected to not join our family. Instead she and her nefarious friends were going to meet with Sgt. Moore's plumpy first wife, who Sgt. Moore had recently divorced for an "upgrade," to discuss the Global Agreement.

While at the coast, my wife called me and exclaimed "YOU ARE NOT GOING TO BELIEVE THIS ... IT'S INCREDIBLE!" She then declared she and her cohorts had figured out a way to finally reconcile her mom and dad, and "get them back on the same team" leveraging the "The Blue House" (discussed in the next chapter).

My wife's idea from a year earlier was to have her Mom move into Blue House, at least until Cire reappeared. This, she explained, would save her Dad from having to pay alimony. And that was increasingly important she said because her Dad now had cancer and would be dying soon. He needed to pay medical bills not covered by health insurance, and her mom needed the security of knowing she would still have shelter after the alimony payments stopped. So Cire's estate moved my wife's abandoned Mom into the Blue house. Still though, and increasingly frustrating for my wife, her parents remained at odds with each other.

My wife's latest idea was now to have her Mom move *out* of the Blue House, and to take our family dog, Bella, with her for company. The only states not yet represented with lawyers in the Global Agreement were Montana (where her Mom and Dad's divorce decree was finalized), North Dakota (where her Dad was now deathly ill) and Minnesota (where an insurance policy my wife had recently obtained covered expenses tied to Bella in case of (i) dog nappings, (ii) catastrophic "vet bills" (ii) and "chip[45]"

---

[45] My wife had a military grade power computer "chip" installed into Bella so that she could track her every move via global position satellites. Literally every single step Bella took, was monitored, recorded and placed into a giant

malfunctions. By stirring up a long standing feud on her side of the family (and requiring her Dad to once again cover her Mom's rent per the Montana divorce decree), moving with our kids to North Dakota to take care of her ailing Dad and adding our "pet pound pup" to the mix, the Global Agreement could involve every state at issue in the Louisiana Purchase, and have universal effect. Even though her antagonistic parents still may not be talking with each other, both of them would be "on the same team" helping Cire's estate wrap up everything with the Global Agreement.

In other words, almost like a miracle, like Jesus reappearing from the dead, my wife's mom and dad were going to be phlegmatically in a boat together, rowing in the same direction. This was now 2015, ten years after such an event was first prophesied in Cire's Gmail account in 2005. Perhaps it was just coincidence, but more likely good foreshadowing, that the email predicting the realignment of my wife's mom and dad was the email following one about a plan for God's to son eventually reclaim and remap the Blue House on Native American land, which Cire's estate had just completed.

---

relational database. Ironically, the tracking my wife was now using with Bella was similar to that used by the US government to monitor its citizens' cell phones. If Bella's chip malfunctioned, or was ever "hacked" (causing Bella to go haywire), that was a "recoverable event" under the terms of the policy.

26

The "Blue House"

The last part of wrapping up Cire's estate involved obtaining the "Blue House" (known as "ground zero" for New America). It was a replacement for Cire's "White House." If Cire was still alive, as my wife continually hinted was likely the case, he could eventually live there. If he was actually dead, the Blue House was still an important acquisition for curing the bank's breach of the Global Agreement regarding demolition of Cire's hacienda, and reconciling Cire's estate.

The "Blue House" is within a stone's throw of mine, on a pristine mountain lake with water clean enough to drink. It is on a lot surrounded by "common area" that the previous owner, a retired New York police officer, notorious for carrying his loaded gun everywhere and living off pension payments tied to 9/11 media events, had adversely possessed. Consequently, after Cire's estate completed the purchase, it ended up with not only the Blue House and underlying lot, but also all the surrounding land.

After Cire passed away, nosey neighbors were interested in the Claim against his estate. The "Blue House" neighbor was especially curious. Part of the reason was that the questionable deeds for Navajo land at issue in the Claim had originated from *the very same police district in New York where he was from* - the precise place Europeans had traded beads to the Native Americans in the 1600's for Manhattan.

The noxious neighbor enjoyed enthusiastically telling the story of how his ancestors had "swindled" the natives out of New York City for a handful of beads, and indeed told that story to Cire when he had first visited our village 2005. The generally gesticulating neighbor was more comatose, however, after hearing Cire explain that his Blue House was "technically" still on native american land, and might eventually someday be reclaimed and remapped. In any event, over the course of many years the aggressive neighbor, always carrying his loaded pistol and on the lookout for natives who he might have to shoot, firmly established dominion over the common areas surrounding his Blue House (including a lakefront beach where natives used to park their canoes). After acquiring the surrounding land (noted for fields of marijuana growing naturally "like weeds" near the lake) he put everything up for sale.

Kaniksu Rocks @KaniksuRocks · Oct 16
NOTICE: Weeds located on tribal land slated to be harvested/burned for common good ...

About this same time Cire's estate was advised that the bank had kicked Cire's agent out of Cire's estate hacienda and was in the process of demolishing it. This was a breach of the Global Agreement. To cure the breach, Cire's estate, at this point being administered by my sprightly sister and our drained uncle[46], obtained the "Blue House" and surrounding land in the name of Cire.

The Global Agreement *releasing all claims from the beginning of time*, signed by appropriate Native American parties and State judges, had effectively made all previous claims, including Statutory ones, affecting the Blue House null and void.

The first "official" New America real estate transaction in our generally quiet village, one that would set an example for future sales, was Cire's estate purchasing the Blue House. After obtaining the "Blue House," Cire's estate provided the public notice of the Global Agreement, and reiterated that all existing maps and claims (including those codified in State statutes and local ordinances) which might otherwise apply to the Blue House and surrounding lands were now null and void, having been superseded by the Global Agreement.

---

[46] After the Global Agreement was signed, I resigned my duties as Personal Representative of Cire's Estate. Afterwards, my sister took over and wrapped everything up, with the help of our uncle.

Cire's estate was starting over with a "blank slate," just as judges from several western states had agreed upon and directed that happen. The only guides governing the Blue House were just the original Constitution and "common sense," which had thousands of years of legal precedence.

As one might imagine this caused quite an uproar with neighbors who were used to doing things (like voting and paying taxes) the old fashion "codified" way, the way they had been doing things for most of their sedentary lives. So it was not just a matter of abolishing all the codified laws (that part was easy and had already been done by virtue of the Global Agreement), it was also a process of educating the bewildered masses on how foolish, and easily manipulatable, their old sluggish system had become.

To start things off Cire's estate attempted to relinquish its ownership of the beach, which had previously been adversely possessed in front of the Blue House, to the village. The goal was to enable all the people -- and their dogs and horses -- to once again enjoy the beach and access the lake. Almost unbelievably, some villagers objected to this. They too had adversely possessed beaches in front of their houses and were uncomfortable with the idea of the "common people" and their animals being able to access the lake.

So a vote was held. But not just any vote. A village vote according to the "old way" of doing things.

In this particular lakefront village the rules which had been interpreted with Animal Farm[47] logic for generations provided that "each lot owner is entitled to a vote." In order to dominate elections, a few large-littered families on the lakefront had claimed to own their lots as "tenancies in common" with each family member being an owner. Thus, according to their interpretation of the rules, each was entitled to a vote. For decades these families of grandparents, aunts, uncles, distant cousins and even a few adopted orphans residing in Africa, held an oligopoly over all elections. They were essentially the lake mafia. They made all the rules to suit their wishes, and enforced them.

Cire's estate solution to this hefty challenge was to "fight fire with fire." If the lakefront mafia was going to have big tenancies in common to dominate the vote, Cire's estate would have an even bigger one.

Soon after Cire's estate established a tenancy in common with an Alphabet Tranche for literally every breathing

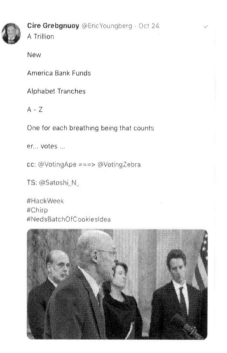

Cire Grebgnuoy @EricYoungberg · Oct 24
A Trillion

New

America Bank Funds

Alphabet Tranches

A – Z

One for each breathing being that counts

er... votes ...

cc: @VotingApe ===> @VotingZebra

TS: @Satoshi_N_

#HackWeek
#Chirp
#NedsBatchOfCookiesIdea

---

[47] Animal Farm (authored by George Orwell and published in 1945) is a book about pigs governing other farm animals.

being[48] on the planet. It was an advanced "Noah's Ark" solution. Every breathing being from a "Voting Ape" to "Voting Zebra" was included and, according to the village's very own interpretation of its election rules, entitled to vote. All of the votes were conveniently consolidated into one trust, a "Trust For Dogs".

Trust For Dogs
@trustfordogs
A Constitutional Voting Trust for Dogs (and all other breathing Beings, sharing clean air, land and water). See @ragnaar. Use @square.

◎ North America   𝒮 sevenplanet.com
▦ Joined April 2017

Ape
@VotingApe
Ape with Voting App. Friends with @ragnaar. Votes via @trustfordogs with sevenplanet.com. A Corporation is a person. #UseSquare #VivaLaFrance

Voting Zebra
@VotingZebra
Friends with Cecil the Lion. Dead. Voted via proxy with @trustfordogs. Now, a corporation, a person, does the voting for Zebras. #UseSquare

---

[48] Most people presumed "all breathing beings" included just the species breathing "air." Cire's estate, however, not taking any chances with losing the vote, established that fish breathing "water" were just as eligible to vote as the "air" breathing beings above ground.

Needless to say, Cire's estate's voters easily won the vote, and the beach was soon after made public again, for the benefit of all of the villagers and animals. New boundless maps were distributed for the village and surrounding lands, and all was good.

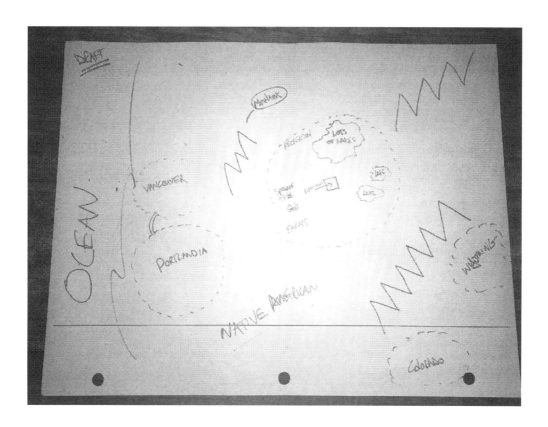

In the short term, for a couple of years afterwards, it was delightful having Cire's estate with its Trust for Dogs in charge. Everything in the village ran smoothly, from the snowplow clearing the village roads in the winter, to the lawnmowers maintaining the village golf course in the summer. And, with volunteer parties (mostly a renegade named "mad dog") harvesting the marijuana on the common land and selling it in the village square, tax revenues were at an all time high.

Long term, though, the villagers were not going to be happy with Cire's estate and its Trust for Dogs dominating every election and vote. Despite villagers living the highest quality of life imaginable, one significantly superior to how they had lived prior to Cire's estate taking over the Blue House and surrounding lands, people were increasingly insistent on wanting to not just reside in, but also participate in the politics of, New America.

For years, Cire's estate and an increasing number of followers had been "living" in the heavenly reality of New America, governed with just the original Constitution and common sense. For these citizens, there was no obligation to file federal income tax returns or pay taxes. What an extraordinarily beautifully simplistic way to live! Others, being unsure of which reality, Old America or New America, "trumped" the other continued to file federal income tax returns, just to be safe.

Patiently, Cire's estate elucidated "New America" to other interested villages. For starters, Cire's estate explained that New America had actually been in existence for quite some time. For some "pure Constitutionalists," like many of those living off the grid, New America (which is "really" Old America) is the only America that has ever existed. New America is a place where one can live "free," without governmental interference or surveillance.

Cire had "launched" (or some might say "relaunched") New America January 1, 2000, (at the start of the new Century and Millenium). Gradually since then more and more people had decided they liked New America better than Old America, and simply informally decided to adopt it as their "country of choice." Then, with the Global Agreement being endorsed by

Old America's judges and appellate judges, all of Old America's claims and post-Constitution codified laws, amendments and Addendums, *including the Bill of Rights,* had simply been made null and void for all those on lands covered by the Global Agreement.

Bottom line is that New America is identical to "really" Old America. It is governed with just the original Constitution and common sense. Its judicial system equitably decides cases based on "common law" with thousands of years of judicial precedent rather than "codified statutes" which oftentimes conflict with, and bastardize, previous decisions of the courts.

Cire's estate further explained that the primary differences between New America and existing Old America -- that most everyone had involuntarily been born into -- involved villages, voting and taxes.

Villages

In New America, villages and villagers have more liberty.

For example, by no longer having a Bill of Rights or a "First Amendment" there are no longer limitations on villages', or villagers', freedom of expression. If a village wants to install a sign promoting the "Ten Commandments" or even a "dead fish" -- they may do so. And if a villager wants to loudly "curse" the sign, they are free to do this also[49]. No longer is "free speech" of a village, or its villagers, restricted, chilled or interfered with by the government.

In New America, a person may say, as my grandmother used to remind us, "whatever they 'damn' well please!"

People may use profanity, and even the "N" word featured in Huckleberry Finn, without fear of being charged with a statutory crime. They can even make "threats" so long as no harm results[50]. Legal recourse against "improper" speech is limited to concepts from common law that pre-date the Constitution, like libel and defamation.

As another example, by no longer having a "Second Amendment" there are no longer procedural methods for the government to sneakily take away a person's right to bear arms. Since the "right to bear arms" was first codified more than two centuries ago, a person's right to defend themselves against the government has slowly been eroded until effectively eliminated in Old

---

[49] A bizarre anomaly of Old America was that freedom of speech became so restricted that it was actually a "crime" to curse loudly.

[50] This is known as the timeless principle of *sticks and stones may break bones but words will never hurt anybody.* It is sickening how many people in Old America have had their freedom taken away for "saying" things verbally or "writing" things online. Every instance of people being placed in custody for "speech" showcases how f'ing pathetic the First Amendment is at protecting free speech.

America. One can lose their right to defend themselves and property with "arms" (which has been broadly and insanely been interpreted to include things like a kid's toy BB gun and even a kitchen knife) for being a felon, acting "crazy" or just by going through a divorce, which affects more than half of the adults in America. In Old America there are so many "carve outs" to the Second Amendment, its functional purpose has essentially been neutered.

In Old America, one may lose the right to a weapon if the weapon or owner is deemed too powerful or risky, respectively. Worse, even if the owner of a weapon still happens to have a Second Amendment right, often they often have to pay a "tax" (disguised as a "permit fee") in order to carry it. If a citizen fails to pay the government required taxes or permit fees, their right to bear *even their own* arms may be infringed upon or even taken away. America's founding fathers would be vomiting at this notion of Old America.

Bottom line is that citizens have more individual liberties in New America. The liberties are identical to those of "really" Old America, founded more than two hundred years ago, which was the reason for founding America in the first place. People can freely speak and bear arms to protect their families, property and villages --- all without federal government interference or taxes.

Voting

In New America, voting is Constitutional.

This one took a while to explain to the elementary villagers, many of whom had become quite accustomed to voting unconstitutionally in Old America. The bottom line is that the United States of America is a "democratic republic" -- not a democracy. The people are not required to vote by the very terms of the Constitution.

People are not expected to vote for the President (that is what the Electors are for) and are actually prohibited from voting for their state's Senators (that is the job of their state Legislators, not the people). The only task the "People" are permitted to participate in at the federal level is "choosing[51]" their Representatives.

Dumbfounded. Awestruck. Stunned.

Those were the general reactions of the villagers who had previously unnecessarily driven great distances, and inconveniently waited in long lines, to cast their votes in Presidential and Senate elections. Once villagers realized they didn't have to vote anymore on these matters "above their pay

---

[51] Although the "choosing" could be accomplished by "votes" it doesn't necessarily have to be

grade" and the system would still work, and indeed work better, just like it was originally designed, a sense of grand relief settled in. Next, after they understood taxes, it was pure jubilation.

Taxes

In New America, taxes are Constitutional.

What does this mean? Well it means that the Federal government is bound to the Constitutional provision that "Taxes <u>shall</u> be apportioned among the several States." In other words, the Federal Government *must tax the states, not the people*.

It is up to the states to figure out how to pay their respective tax bills. Sure states might tax their people, and pass those funds along the federal government. But, not necessarily. Some states might just sell natural resources (for example sustainably harvested trees on state land) to meet their yearly tax burden. In any event it is the responsibility of the states, not the people, to fund the federal government.

Sheer ecstasy. Nirvana. Shangri la. That was how the villagers described it.

America was the best place. Ever. New America was exactly as Old America was first imagined. A place where people could live free, with the greatest of liberties and without a federal income tax on individuals.

Locally in the villages taxes are effectively "voluntary" with villages electing to "tax themselves" or not. For villages that do decide to tax themselves, the taxes vary widely from village to village. Some villages have all kinds of taxes -- ranging from property taxes, to sales taxes, to gross receipts taxes, to value added taxes to a mix of everything -- and effectively tax their citizens until death (and sometimes even afterwards). Other villages don't have any taxes.

 If villagers want to "make improvements" to their village they can tax themselves, accept donations (like a church), volunteer to do the work themselves, or use a combination. In the end, like always, the "golden rule"[52] prevails.

To help the village understand with a real life example, a controversial new "road less traveled" and "horse bridge to town" (collectively, "the Road") was proposed.

Some villagers did not want the Road. This "don't change anything" group consisted of people unwilling to help with the proposed project in any

---

[52] The golden rule provides that "those who have the gold make the rules (and roads and bridges)."

manner. They were not going to pay any new taxes, donate funds or volunteer any of their time or resources to help complete the Road.

On the other side was a "pro-development" group. They wanted the Road so badly that they were willing to complete it all by themselves, without any help from the "don't change anything" group. They would use a mixture of existing Old America tax dollars already in reserve, donated New America funds (with a fair market value of $100,000), and volunteer resources to make the Road a reality.

With the simple application of the golden rule, and despite objections from the "don't change anything" group" which the "pro development group" effectively steam rolled, the Road improvements are presently underway for the benefit of everyone in the village.

Blue House Resolution

After learning more about villages, voting, and taxes -- and seeing application of the golden rule in action -- many villagers, especially those high on "cloud nine" with Mad Dog, were as happy as "stink on skunk."

To make things even better, Cire's estate then explained that the boatloads of corporations in its Alphabet Tranche (consolidated with a "Trust for Dogs") were actually **not** people.[53] Consequently, they would no longer be participating in the political process. Cire's estate was effectively taking "big money" out of politics.

The only money in politics going forward would be a nominal "poll tax" to help keep track of the *people* voting. The poll tax was fixed at one roundUp per vote. RoundUps, or some might say "votes", could be purchased with whatever currency a voter happened to favor -- from Old America Federal Reserve Notes, to Mexican Pesos, to Canadian Loonies, to even Bitcoin, all based on the then-current exchange values.

From that point on, operating on the principle of "Just do Nothing" this independent and self-sufficient New America village was at peace, and remains so. No Wars. No Standing Army. No Gitmo.

---

[53] This of course ran contrary to the precedent of the Old America Supreme court, which by virtue of a headnote included in an opinion written by a young clerk, had earlier decided that indeed "a corporation is a person."

People in the village govern themselves, locally. They voluntarily coordinate snowplow efforts in the winter, and improve the parks in the summer. All peacefully.

After the village updated from Old America to New America the quality of life improved noticeably for every breathing being[54], all sharing clean water, clean air and living peacefully. Capitalizing on the "Blue House" Cire's estate had effectively established a scalable working model for a supremely peaceful America.

---

[54] It is worth a footnote, and perhaps even a book someday, to mention that in Old America villagers were known for obtaining "permits" to execute animals. With a high powered rifle and permit it was possible and even legal to "explode the brains" right out of the skull of one of God's creatures smack dab in the middle of the village. Eventually understanding that it was indeed possible for the animals, properly organized and represented in their Trusts, to issue similar permits on the people, a mutual understanding was reached in the village that reflected God's will perfectly: "Thou shall not kill." Villagers who previously encouraged their sons to slaughter and skin the village animals for sport now, somewhat sheepishly like little lambs, encouraged their offspring to refrain from harming any breathing being in the village for fear if they were not careful going forward, they themselves could be slaughtered and skinned, with a properly issued permit.

27

America

America (North and South) is an immense landmass with the natural borders of the Pacific Ocean on one side, and the Atlantic Ocean on the other.

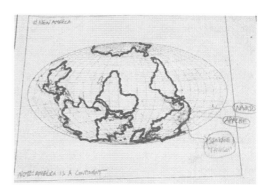

And just like everywhere else in the world, America has people who generally and naturally self-organize into villages. Villages are places where people know each other, and share common interests (like peace and domestic tranquility). They are also places that typically offer everything needed for their villagers to survive[55].

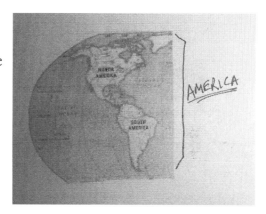

---

[55] These are often referred to as the "sevens." That is, the seven categories of consumer goods generally every villager on the planet needs to comfortably survive. Namely, apparel, energy, food, health, household (items), shelter and travel.

Historically, villages in America were more rural, with residents often living a day or more away by horseback ride into the village center. Today, villages are increasingly urban and are often clustered tightly together. In a big metropolitan city there may be countless villages, so overlapped it can be impossible to tell where one starts and another begins.

Sure, these geographic collections of people are often called by various names -- suburbs, beaches, districts, high-rise buildings, communities, pueblos, reservations or even zip codes -- and they may be urban or rural, but all, at their heart, are villages.

America, from sea to shining sea, is essentially just a big collection of villages. Some villages, indeed most, have sprung into existence since the founding of the United States, mostly due to massive population increases everywhere. Others though, historic Native American villages for example, have peacefully existed for many hundreds of years, well before the white men "settled" America.

After the tiny slice of America's eastern seaboard was first conquered and mapped with thirteen states of villages, the Constitution was adopted. The expectation then, just as it is today, was that villages all over America would be organized into "states" governed with, and protected by, the Constitution.

There was no limit then, just as there is no limit now, on the precise number of states. The only limitation is a geographical one contained in the Constitution limiting states to those of "America."

Over time, America, with its expanding number of villages and states has been mapped and remapped. Likely, as people continue to refine and improve how they self-organize and govern themselves, America will be remapped, again and again.

There is nothing in the Constitution that mandates that states be huge, defined by linear boundaries or even connected. In many ways having hundreds (or more) smaller disconnected states and self-governing Native American Nations sprinkled across America makes a lot more sense than having fifty mostly giant states (now including one in the Pacific ocean) generally separated with arbitrary grid lines.

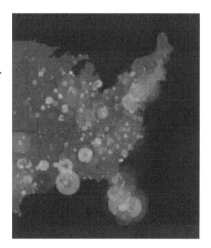

These fundamental principles were taught in Cire's high school classes, with vintage paper maps hanging from the walls. For Cire and his classmates, the notion of America being

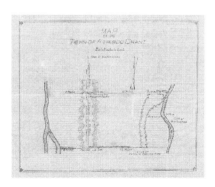

continually remapped was self-evident by the very school they attended. The school campus was on Navajo Nation Land (starting with the "beginning of time"), which was later settled as the "Sandia" Reservation" (about 300 BC), which was later claimed as a Spanish Land Grant (in 1848 AD) before being declared to be part of New Mexico (1912). Like lots of land in America, the school's property has a history of bitterly contested ownership, which has changed over time and which may continue to evolve.

In any event, that is what Cire was taught and preached. America is a Continent of villages, which has been, and will continue to be remapped. The once constant going forward, even as the number of states naturally fluctuates, is that all of the villages of America, and all of her citizens, will be governed by, and protected with, the Constitution.

28

The Constitution

The Constitution of the United States of America is the most perfect document ever drafted. With just seven simple Articles, and punctuated with a "done" at the end[56], it effectively enables an unlimited number of states, villages and citizens to collectively thrive in peace. All this is accomplished with a carefully layered, balanced, democratic republic form of self-government.

Before drafting the Constitution, its founders carefully reviewed, considered and debated all the great works of history including The Bible (Old[57] and New[58] Testaments), The Koran[59] and The Magna Carta[60].

---

[56] Of significance, the "done" has the same large font size as the Article headings. In other words, "seven articles and done".
[57] 1600 to 400 BC
[58] 367 AD
[59] 609 to 632 AD
[60] 1215 AD

The goal of the Constitution was to create the best form of peaceful, scalable, inclusive government possible -- one that was better than anything previously invented and one that would naturally stand the test of time. In the end, this was achieved, perfectly, with *just* the original Constitution.

Sure Old America still kinda "works" with a Bill of Rights and the other cumbersome Addendums, it just doesn't work as well. It is less peaceful than ideal, and absolute individual rights in Old America (for example, freedom of speech) can be infringed upon thus proving how ineffective the Bill of Rights actually is at protecting rights.

Of course the Constitution may be amended. And it may be unamended. It is just not supposed to have things "addended" to it.

Jefferson wrote the original Constitution protecting individual freedoms *implicitly*. He viewed the Bill of Rights to the United States Constitution as unnecessary (otherwise he would have added them to the Constitution himself) and a threat to the very individual liberties the Constitution was intending to protect.

These principles were discussed and repeated among Cire's friends while in high school. During their senior year they had all been selected to attend a weeklong student government event at the New Mexico State Capitol in

Santa Fe[61]. On the final evening, Cire and friends celebrated the Constitution while toasting several cheerleaders from a rival school with shots of tequila in their suites.

The class valedictorian was in charge of pouring drinks, and summing everything up. He explained to anyone willing to listen or wanting more tequila that the Constitution is a bit like a finely crafted high-performance 911 Porsche Targa. It is OK to amend it (for example "swap the wheels"). It just shouldn't have things addended to it (for example "have a horse trailer hooked up to it with a tow hitch).

Sure, it may be able to function with extra burden for a while. But it would not perform as well and, eventually, would break down. To fix it, whatever it was towing should be removed, and the broken parts replaced with genuine originals.

The constitutional conversations continued with Cire doing most of the listening. A casual understanding was soon reached that the first 100 years of the United States was generally politically uneventful, except for a growing consensus among political savants that the Constitution's Addendums should eventually be abolished in the interest of unbridled individual freedoms.

---

[61] A village established in 1610 by the Spanish conquistador Oñate after heading north along the Rio Grande from Bravo Farms.

Discussions of the next 100 years, filled with increasingly nonsensical Addendums and World Wars, were louder. Cire and his classmates considered the Addendums and wars to be interrelated and, combined, a foolish waste of time, energy and lives. "To get rid of the wars, get rid of the Addendums." That was what Cire's highschool class had been taught, and what Cire and his friends, old and new, preached ever after.

More than two hundred years ago Jefferson cautioned against burdening the Constitution with a Bill of Rights or other silly Addendums. He could foresee with perfectly clarity what is now reality. These unnecessary dead weights would increasingly be exploited by bullies intent on strong arming and twisting a lean "government of peace" into a mean and heavy "business at war." Moreover, slowly but steadily, individual liberties implicitly protected the Constitution (like being able to speak freely, assemble freely, practice religion freely and defend one's property and rights freely) would steadily be corroded and eroded until they were explicitly eliminated, just as is the case today in Old America.

The Addendums are a "ball and chain" for every citizen. They restrict, impede and limit individual freedoms and liberty. They unfortunately have accomplished the exact opposite of their stated purpose. Rather than protect individual rights, they have effectively suppressed them.

When this inevitably happened, as Thomas Jefferson accurately anticipated it would, the federal government would naturally fail, being bankrupt both morally and fiscally, just as it is today. Upon the collapse of the federal government, Jefferson advised people not to fret but rather to simply start over with *just* the original Constitution, precisely as the people in Cire's village, and all those on the lands subject to the Global Agreement, had done with New America.

The Constitution was intended to allow villages of people to harmoniously coexist and peacefully "self-govern." Every village is different. Each is geographically unique and has its own culture. And, at the same time, every village is identical in its desire for its inhabitants to live happy, peaceful and satisfying lives.

The Constitution enables all villages of America, no matter how different with respect to their people, religions, customs and languages, to peacefully thrive together with a representative form of self-governance. The Constitution, through a federal government, connects these villages with a Post Office, roads, infrastructure, common interests and defense.

Other than that, each of the villages, and all of their inhabitants are free and blessed with virtually unlimited personal liberties to the extent they don't harm others. In other words, one person's "right" to throw a punch stops at another person's face.

The only restrictions on personal liberties are those which are "common sense." And, fortunately, for thousands of years common sense has been documented with common law. So now, all citizens in villages everywhere have access to "common sense" in case of doubt.

As an example, is it OK to yell "fire" in a crowded movie theater?

Of course it is !

If there actually was a fire, the statement was likely a helpful warning. If there wasn't a fire, though, perhaps the statement was just a joke or obvious "fake news." Nevertheless, if someone actually got hurt running out of the theater because of the inaccurate statement, whoever yelled "fire" *might* have liability under common law, presuming whoever ran was acting reasonably. The point is that common law already more than sufficiently covers free speech, and its limitations.

Importantly, common law does a far better job of protecting *all* individual liberties with common sense, rather than just a few limited ones codified in the "laundry list" of the Bill of Rights and other Addendums. This was a primary reason Jefferson did not include the "silly" Bill of Rights with the original Constitution. It is also a reason that Cire's village is able to now peacefully exist with its citizens enjoying the greatest degree of personal liberties imaginable -- governed with just the Original Constitution.

Tribe 3 🔒 @ISISofAmerica · 2/19/18   ⌄
Hey Hey :)

You said something Unconstitutional...

#WheresWaldo

Cc: @senjudiciary @edgett

#CrackOfTheBat
#SavannaPublicLibrary

At the conclusion of Cire's highschool student government exercises, parties agreed that it would make sense to run two Americas in parallel -

- Old America, burdened with the Bill of Rights and two centuries of additional codified "nonsense," and
- New America, operating frictionlessly with just the original Constitution and "common sense".

Following that Cire strived for a peaceful New America, a collection of decentralized villages governed with just the original Constitution. As New America was increasingly successful, with its inhabitants living happier lives with more liberties and less tax, its villages would "naturally" replicate and thrive.

Cire "forked" the two Americas ("Old and New") on the last day of the last millennium. They have been running in parallel ever since. Eventually, and soon if Cire's Master Plan unfolds according to schedule, New America will effectively completely trump Old America.

Again, a primary difference between New America and Old America is that the Constitution for New America, which is identical to the Constitution for "really" Old America, doesn't recognize the silly amendments or "Addendums" to the Constitution. Other than that, they are similar. Both still have seven Articles, the first one of which establishes Congress.

29

Congress

The Constitution's first order of business, Article 1, establishes Congress. The size of Congress is flexible. It can be small, with just a few states participating, or gargantuan, with a limitless number of states participating.

Notably, the Constitution does not provide for a Capitol *building* for Congress. Instead it provides for a *district* (now known as the District of Columbia) <u>not to exceed ten square miles</u> for the seat of government. Originally the expectation seems to have been that Congress would assemble not in a formal building[62] for long periods of time, but rather yearly[63] in a park-like setting more like an outdoor festival with campfires right after Thanksgiving.

In any event, Congress consists of two chambers, each with its own unique set of responsibilities:

---

[62] In the early 1800's some people built the first Capitol Building, to be maintained at taxpayer expense. Others burned it to the ground.

[63] The actual language was/is "The Congress shall assemble at least once in every Year, and such Meeting shall be on the first Monday in December, unless they shall by Law appoint a different Day."

- The House of Representatives, where all Bills for raising Revenue originate, and
- The Senate, which approves (or disapproves) Bills from the House of Representatives.

House of Representatives

The rules for selecting Members of the The House of Representatives are identical in both Old America and New America.

The original Constitution provides that the House of Representatives *"shall be composed of Members chosen every second Year by the* **__People__**[64] *of the several States."*

This Constitutional provision has never been changed by amendment or attempted to be overridden by Addendum. The method for selecting Members to the House of Representatives remains in its pure, unadulterated, original form in both Old America and New America. Members are chosen by "People" -- all colors, genders and, arguably, even ages.

---

[64] Emphasis, both bold and underline, has been added to reinforce that the Constitution uses the expansive, and non-discriminatory word of "People." The Constitution does not favor one color, gender or age over another. "People are people" as the saying goes, and includes every living human being.

Additionally it is worth noting that the Constitution doesn't specifically say the Members shall be chosen by "vote" or that "only those who have reached the age of majority may vote," although that is how we have been doing things for over two hundred years. Theoretically, states could choose their representative members randomly (like with a lottery), or based on a time-honored game of a skill (like chess, or golf), and that still would seem to be acceptable in terms of the Constitution.

The rules for choosing Members of the House of Representative have remained the same since the Constitution's earliest days. In other words, when people follow the Constitution and choose their Representatives every second year, they are precisely following the Constitution, in both New America and Old America.

The Senate

The rules are different for determining Senators in New America and Old America.

The original Constitution, the one governing New America, establishes that the Members of the Senate are *not* to be voted into office by the general public, or even selected by them in any manner at all. The original Constitution provides:

"The Senate of the United States shall be composed of two Senators from each State, <u>chosen by the Legislature</u> thereof..." (emphasis added)

This provision, crucial for making sure America remains a stable democratic republic and not a whimsical "pure democracy," was overridden in Old America in 1913 with the 17th Addendum which provides:

The Senate of the United States shall be composed of two Senators from each State, <u>elected by the people</u> thereof, for six years (emphasis added)

This is perhaps the most significant, and problematic, change that has ever been made to the Constitution of Old America.

A fundamental purpose of the Senate is to allow legislation from the House of Representatives resulting from the hot tempers of the people to "cool." In order to properly, and safely, do their jobs Senators are supposed to be insulated, one step removed, from the often temperamental will of the people.

Thomas Jefferson once described Congress as a cup of tea. The People were like scalding hot tea. The House of Representatives was like the tea cup, which kept everyone contained, even when boiling hot. The Senate was like the saucer, which safely held both until the tea was cool enough to drink.

The 17th Addendum, in and of itself, radically changed Old America's system of government from a carefully balanced, strongly interwoven, democratic republic to virtually a pure democracy (also known as "mob rule"), which great thinkers since the time of the collapse of the Roman Empire have cautioned against. The change in how Senators are selected would not have been acceptable to our founders. They would have undoubtedly seen the 17th Addendum for what it is, a further sabotaging of the very principles upon which our country was founded -- perhaps another step towards convincing everyone to get rid of the "Addendums" altogether and simply start over with just the original Constitution[65].

Powers of Congress

The Constitution provides Congress a detailed list of powers to achieve the goal of "domestic tranquility" otherwise known as "peace."

Since the first hostilities of western civilization in Greece thousands of years ago, the world has been at war. The Constitution's founders were trying to change this. They were striving to achieve the elusive notion of lasting peace for everyone in America, those dealing with her and eventually everywhere else.

---

[65] Perhaps it is no coincidence that the "next" Addendum, the 18th which outlawed beer and was soon after abolished with the 21st Addendum, was the first successful "proof of concept" that Addendums can indeed be eliminated.

The most peaceful places are, obviously, those least warlike. Ideally, a country would never be at a war and, consequently, never need an army. Of course, if a country is ever invaded it might be helpful to have lots of folks interested in defending their land armed with weapons. In this regard America has always been in great shape.

With a view towards peace, the Constitution specifically prohibits long-term standing armies. In extraordinary circumstances, an appropropriation for a short term, two-year, army is permitted. That is it though. Just two years.

If the Representatives (who are passing Bills to fund a war) can't figure out how to end a war in two years, it is time to replace them with new Representatives who can. The two year limitation, for standing armies and terms of Representative funding the armies, is more than just coincidence. It is a thoughtful strategy for peace through economics.

Old America has had not *two*, but rather, *two hundred* years of standing armies. It has fought everything from "World Wars" to "Wars on Drugs[66]" to "Wars with Terrorists[67]". ALL of these wars exceed the constitutional limits for a standing army and, perhaps more importantly, have effectively bankrupted Old America's Treasury.

---

[66] Presumably first coined in Vietnam, where soldiers partied with marijuana while surfing nice Asian beaches
[67] Terrorists are people "saying" things which are frightening.

Jefferson used to say "if a Country engages in long-term wars it will eventually find itself broken, both morally and fiscally." Old America is now broken, morally and fiscally. That is why New America started over.

Unlike Old America, New America does not have a standing army. No funds have been allocated to an army because an army has never been needed. There are already more privately-owned weapons than people in New America. Any country which tried to take over New America by force would likely face armed volunteers far greater in number and strength than any Old America army.

That being said, New America, like Old America, does have a Navy. The Constitution provides that Congress shall have power to provide and maintain a Navy. For a sense of domestic security, it is expected that the Navy will protect America's shores, waterways and maritime lines of commerce.

There is, however, one critical difference between the Navy of Old America and that of New America. Old America's Navy is maintained at taxpayer expense. New America's Navy is maintained with volunteers. Together, the taxpayers of Old America and volunteers of New America have effectively kept the waters of America and surrounding lands safe for as long as most can remember.

In summary, the Constitution establishes Congress, articulates the procedures for selecting its Members and provides a detailed list of its powers. The Constitution does not, however, say anything about people "voting" for Members of Congress.

This leads us to our next topic -- one that Cire reminded me of the last time we visited in the rose garden of his new "White House" -- the Constitutional procedure for selecting the President.

30

President

Article II of the Constitution provides for a President.

It articulates that "*The executive Power shall be vested in a President of the United States of America*[68]."

Similar to Article I (providing rules for selecting Members of Congress), Article II does <u>not</u> provide for a "vote of the people."

New America's Constitution (the "original Constitution") mandates that the President is chosen by *Electors*, who are appointed by the States. Old America's Constitution (the original Constitution since modified with all kinds of asinine amendments and Addendums, including the 12th) also mandates that the President is chosen by Electors, but changes the process mostly with respect to how "Vice" Presidents are selected.

---

[68] Importantly, this says "America." It does not say "World." It also does not say "America and the Pacific Islands." The Constitution's preamble limits the United States to the geographic scope of the continent of "America." Article II reinforces this geographic boundary.

As difficult as it may be to believe for many citizens of present-day America, some of whom have been voting for President since last reciting the Pledge of Allegiance in highschool, there is no provision in the Constitution that a President will be elected into office by a "vote" of the people. According to the Constitution, for both New America and Old America, Electors vote for the President. Ordinary citizens do *not* vote for the President.

This was the revelation that Cire's estate shared with New America villages that brought great joy to the citizens. No longer did they have to drive great distances or wait in long lines for something they were not expected to do in the first place. When Old America villagers asked New America villagers why they didn't vote for the President, they simply replied "according to the Constitution we aren't supposed to vote, and neither are you."

Another important clause of the Constitution, which has never changed, and thus is the same in New America and Old America, provides "*No Person except a natural born Citizen, or a Citizen of the United States, at the time of the Adoption of this Constitution, shall be eligible to the Office of President.*"

What exactly does this mean?

Well, it means what it says.

Ask any good Constitutional Law scholar, or grammatarian, and they will tell you that the only people in the modern era who are eligible to be President are those "naturally born." Humans born through artificial insemination (like a racehorse) at any time *after* the adoption of the Constitution, are not eligible to be President. In the long run, the founders wanted people who were "God's creations" to be President, not "human experiments."

At the time the Constitution was being drafted, some of those helping negotiate its provisions were suspected to have been carefully bred by unnatural means due to their extraordinarily gifted talents. This was especially true of Hamilton who was known to be an orphan "without a father." To accommodate the possibility of Hamilton (or any of the other country's founders without a father) being President, a clause was added allowing that for anyone then living, they did not have to be "naturally born" to be eligible to be President. They just had to be a citizen of one of the original thirteen states at the time the Constitution was adopted.

Some radical Constitutional theorists have taken liberty with interpretation of eligibility and concluded that only natural born citizens from the original thirteen states are eligible to be President today. This line of logic is refuted by the precise language in the Constitution's preamble, which is reinforced with Article II, establishing the geographical boundaries as to where a President may be born as any State on the continent of "America."

Thus a citizen naturally born anywhere on the continent of America that is within a State is eligible to be President. Someone born on a different continent (like Africa) or island in the middle of the ocean (like Hawaii), however, is technically ineligible to be President for geographical reasons, as set forth in the Constitution.

This was a conversation topic that Cire and his New America political friends loved discussing. In their view, the result of the Presidential election of 2008, the last one before Cire passed away, was invalid.

According to identical rules in play for both New America and Old America, the person chosen to be President in 2008 was ineligible by the very terms of the Constitution. This of course presented a monumental challenge, especially since a tsunami of "voters" had elected Barack Obama (from Hawaii, by way of Kenya) to serve as President. It also presented the opportunity of a lifetime, for both America and the Chief Justice of the U.S. Supreme Court.

Some background history is in order here. In the election of 2000, just after New America and Old America "forked," two candidates for President each received the most "votes" depending on which way the votes were counted. This highlighted how faulted America's election process had become. By not following the Constitutional procedure for selecting a President, America was unable to decide who was in charge and was rapidly becoming the "joke of democracy." For a royal punchline, rather than have Electors choose the President as they were Constitutionally required to do, the Supreme Court Chief Justice, who had been appointed to his position by George Bush I, handpicked George Bush II, to serve as President. With one fell swoop of the gavel, Old America instantaneously changed from a democratic republic to a virtual monarchy.

Truly hilarious. It also, however, had profound practical effects. It simultaneously signaled an eventual "end" to Old America and "beginning" of New America.

Like all Presidents, the Supreme Court Justices take an oath to "protect and defend the Constitution." The Oath is limited to "just" the Constitution. It does not include protecting and defending any of the "Addendums."

The Addendums are de facto unconstitutional. The constitution permits amendments, not Addendums. The Supreme Court Justices have no say whatsoever in burdensome Addendums suffocating the Constitution (the Constitution that they have sworn to "protect and defend") until, of course, they have the final say.

After the 2000 election Chief Justice Roberts made a courageous decision. He agreed, even though it was unconstitutional to do so, to choose the President ("his choice") to save the country.

After the 2008 election, Chief Justice Roberts made an even more courageous decision. It was, and will likely remain, the greatest act of bravery in the history of the United States. He would expand the definition of "America."

Hawaii, in the middle of the Pacific ocean, is not America. And, despite Congress having claimed that it has indeed been a part of America since 1959, does not make it so. Although the precise question had never reached the Supreme Court, the answer is easy. If Hawaii can be a State, then virtually anywhere else, no matter how far from the Continent of America can be a State. Israel can be a State. Even the moon can be a State.

Chief Justice Robert's expansion of the definition of America to include places not on the Continent, made America unlimited. It could literally go to the far side of the Universe and back. Bold thinking indeed.

As a practical matter, expanding the definition of America would solve several issues, easily and all at once.

- Long term, or perhaps more accurately, "eventually," it would avoid the Supreme Court from having to explain to Congress, and "voters," that Hawaii is not America. Better to let them all save face.

- Mid-term it would enable America to potentially pick up all kinds of other distant places off the continent already "targeted" as states without Constitutional challenge. Puerto Rico (where Cire's ocean liner was docked), Guam, the Philippines, Cuba, Israel, Afghanistan, Iran, Iraq, and even the Cook Islands could all easily be states.
- Short term, and perhaps most importantly, it would allow Barack Obama, who was otherwise constitutionally ineligible, whether born in Kenya or Hawaii, to act as President.

The Chief Justice, single-handedly effectively expanding "America" to the outer edges of the universe for all time was brilliantly heroic.

What he would do next though was even more awe inspiring.

In addition to broadening America to the greatest spatial limits imaginable, the Chief Justice was going to (i) "bury" unconstitutional Old America and (ii) "give life" to constitutional New America. Most impressively, and graciously, he was going to put in his long-time Harvard Law School arch-rival Barack Obama in charge of both tasks.

Barack Obama, a former Senator and constitutional law professor, and John Roberts, the Chief Justice of the US Supreme Court were both quite familiar with the Constitution (obviously). And now, more than ever, they each increasingly understood the importance and transitioning unconstitutional Old America to constitutional New America in a peaceful manner. The dilemma was how to best just do it.

The solution was Cire's. Simply run BOTH Americas, Old America (unconstitutional and broke with $14 Trillion in deficits) and New America (constitutional and flush with $14 Trillion in surplus roundUps) in parallel and let the best one (New America, which is actually "really" Old America) win. The mission was flawless.

To initiate the undertaking, Chief Justice Roberts administered *two* oaths of office to Barack Obama. The first, for Old America, was jumbled, and taken literally, required Barack to "execute faithfully" unconstitutional Old America. Barack took the oath -- hook, line and sinker.

The second oath, for New America, was clean, precise and Constitutional. It is the same oath George Washinton took for "really" Old America -- before there were silly amendments or Addendums to the Constitution. It is as follows:

> *"I do solemnly swear that I will ... to the best of my Ability, preserve, protect and defend the Constitution of the United States."*

Barack Obama would effectively be pulling double duty, acting as President for both Americas. He would be one of the last Presidents of Old America. And he would be the first "official" President of New America.

He would be entrusted to "bury" warring Old America with increasing debt and "unamerican" ideas like "mandatory health insurance" included in an unconstitutional tax code. He would do all this from the Old America White House and, to emphasize how unconstitutional Old America had become, would periodically direct a robot to unconstitutionally sign expenditure bills for him.

Simultaneously, he would be nurturing a peaceful "New America," mostly from a golf course. He would encourage people, villages and states to responsibly take care of themselves with what was coined as the radical idea of "self-government." New America would simply follow the already successfully proven principles in Cire's village of "Just do Nothing." No wars. No locking up people for things they have said. No expenditure from the Treasury[69] unless such expenditure is actually Constitutional -- properly in the form of a Bill from the House of Representatives, approved by the Senate and signed by the actual President (not a robot).

Barack Obama was a wonderful President for Old America, and remains so for New America.

He successfully buried Old America in hell with unforgivable debts. And, he made sure the entire world was aware how bankrupt morally and fiscally Old America had become fighting nonsensical wars overseas and locking people at GITMO (and sometimes even parking lots) for things they had said.

For New America, Barack Obama started off with a Treasury surplus of $14 Trillion roundUps, which remains available today. Volunteers in New America did everything the country and villages needed, or that Barack

---

[69] As a somewhat ironic twist of fate, on the weekend before Barack was sworn into office the US Government unconstitutionally hacked into @ragnaar's twitter account and downloaded documentation for $14 Trillion roundUps These roundUps are New America's Treasury.

Obama ever asked of them. New America was at peace with the world, and remains so, just like the Constitution's founders hoped would someday be the case. And, given that there are no term limits in New America, Barack Obama may continue in his role as President until a replacement is properly selected and sworn into office . If he resigns before then, his Vice-President naturally will take over, just like the Constitution provides.

The last election for a President of Old America, the last one ever according to Cire's Master Plan, was in 2016. Like other Old America elections, it was hilariously unconstitutional.

Eight years earlier, in 2008, Barack Obama had received a majority of the votes to be President of Old America yet was *technically* ineligible absent a radical expansion of the definition of America, which the Chief Justice heroically had managed to achieve. In 2016, Hillary Clinton received a majority of the votes to be President of Old America, yet was *absolutely* ineligible.

The Constitution provides that "People" (which includes all genders) select their Representatives. With regard to the Presidency, however, the Constitution specifically and precisely provides that "He" (not "she" or the "President," but rather "He" with capital "H") "shall hold the office [of President]." In other words, *Mrs.* Clinton was ineligible to be President.

Chief Justice John Roberts was arguably the most powerful, accomplished and clever person in America after expanding the definition of "America" to enable Barack to become President. He was still just human though. Changing the interpretation of "He" to "she" would take an Act Of God, or at least a decision from the Supreme Court, which had not yet happened.

The 2016 "race" for President was, thus, between an ineligible candidate (Mrs. Clinton) who ended up receiving the most votes, and a businessman (Mr. Trump) known for his expertise in restructuring complex bankruptcies and objecting to Old America's unconstitutional tax. Since the very race itself was unconstitutional (because the "race" had just one eligible candidate, it was not actually a race, but rather more of a "fun run"), the result was as well.

The Supreme Court was already contemplating this "perfect storm" of constitutional chaos when rumors arrived that the Russians were trying to "hack the elections" of Old America. This was perhaps the most entertaining, and ludicrous, storyline of modern politics.

The Constitution, by establishing that Electors from the States select the President, ensures a carefully interwoven approach to its democratic republic form of self-government. In other words, the Russians (or whoever else) can try to hack the elections in America all they want. As long as the allegiances of the Electors remain true to the States (which they of course do, because

Electors are guided at the most fundamental level by their own State's "self interest") the President is always representative of the States, even if some of the States and/or their Electors are influenced to a degree by foreign interests.

In any event, New America was working beautifully perfectly. It was at peace and self-governing frictionlessly with just the original Constitution.

Meanwhile, Old America was "done." It was broken beyond repair and acting increasingly unconstitutionally. Adding to its problems, Old America was now in a panic over the Russians possibly influencing the elections. It was a perfect time to transition even more of Old America to New America.

In 2008, the *Chief* Justice of the Supreme Court eloquently transitioned the acting President of the United States from Old America to New America. Now, in 2016, the most *senior* Justice of the Supreme Court would stealthily, yet just as effectively, do the same for the Supreme Court. He would transition the acting Supreme Court from Old America to New America.

31

Supreme Court

The Constitution, in Article III, establishes a Supreme Court. It does not set a minimum (or maximum) number of Justices to sit on its bench. There can be zero, one, a few, or an unlimited number of Supreme Court Justices.

In the months leading up to the 2016 election people were polarized between Old America (which still had not completed Barack Obama's first executive order issued in 2009 to "Close Gitmo"[70]) and New America (which does not have term limits for Presidents, effectively enabling a President to stay in office indefinitely).

There were strong arguments of why Barack Obama would continue as President of New America with just the original Constitution. He was the preeminent leader of America. He spoke for the people. In the approaching times of inevitable chaos, America was going to look to Obama for guidance.

---

[70] Gitmo was a Constitutional hot potato. People were being locked up and subject to cruel and unusual punishment for "free speech" violations. The President had ordered GITMO closed. His military and Congress had refused (thus arguably engaging in Treason). Eventually the Supreme Court would likely have to play a role in protecting and defending the integrity of the Constitution, and the right to free speech.

Perhaps most importantly however, there had not yet been a Constitutional election to replace him. So, much to the chagrin of his critics, Barack was indeed still President of New America.

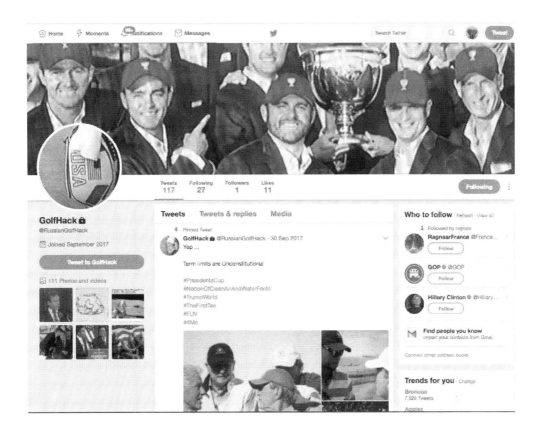

Some of course, mostly those who had been brainwashed with Old America and still could recite the Pledge of Allegiance from heart, argued that the story of Obama being President of New America, and even New America itself, was just "fake news." It was just a big media production kinda like "The West Wing" or "House of Cards." Although it may be entertaining to imagine a perfectly constitutional country of villages -- with a $14 Trillion operating surplus and citizens enjoying unlimited personal liberties expanding as far as "common sense" -- it was not "real," at least not for everyone.

After reviewing the paperwork from Cire's New America village (just the original Constitution and Treasury roundUps) they conceded New America might be "real" for the people in Cire's estate village, and even those in neighboring villages sharing roads and bridges, but until it was broadcast across the country on the evening news (just like 9/11 and the Boston Marathon), it was not real for everyone. Until then, it was just more debatable "fake news."

About this same time, New America websites and Old America televisions began reporting that the longest presiding member of the Supreme Court, Justice Antonin Scalia, had surprisingly passed away. Scalia, the most senior justice on the bench having served since last century, was reported dead at a Texas bird ranch with a shotgun and feather pillow over his head.

When Cire passed away his "Political View" was on the nightstand. When Scalia passed away a copy of just the original Constitution (without any amendments or Addendums) was duct-taped to the wall. This had been provided to Scalia by President Ronald Reagan who had appointed Scalia to the Supreme Court of Old America. It was, and is, the foundation for New America.

For Scalia and other constitutional "purists," the idiotic amendments and Addendums to the Constitution, and especially the one establishing an income tax responsible for funding wars all over the world, had destroyed Old America.

At a dinner (featuring bacon-wrapped dove with jalapeno, served on a rustic hardwood table) the night before Scalia was "called in"[71] as dead, he reportedly shared the hilarious story of Cire's New America village, which had expanded voting rights all the way to the virtually absurd (where "every breathing being" could theoretically vote, through proxy) and then very practically had reverted to reality, of being governed with just the original Constitution and common sense.

---

[71] Scalia's passing brought to light the notion of Habeas Corpus. The coroner who declared Scalia dead never actually saw Scalia dead. The coroner had just heard on a phone call that Scalia had died after a night of heavy laughing.

Tribe 3

@ISISofAmerica

Citizens following Constitution providing a vote for all eligible. See @sevenplanet @KaniksuRocks. Use @Square Credit @VotingBird.

⊙ Europe 𝒮 twitter.com
◔ Born on December 6, 1965
▦ Joined June 2016

100 Following **40** Followers

Scalia was increasingly aware that the Supreme Court was overworked, and mostly busy on completely silly cases about the even sillier Bill of Rights. He also understood that a Supreme Court would operate more efficiently "unburdened" from having to consider issues related to the never-ending "noise" of Old America's Addendums. Collectively, the Addendums starting with the Bill of Rights had proven themselves unsuccessful for more than 200 years at their intended purpose of limiting the size and reach of the Government. Further they had not protected individual liberties but, rather, virtually abolished them.

Pulling the trigger for New America was an easy choice for Scalia, for several reasons including the following -

- First, Scalia, and eventually anyone else on the New America Supreme Court, was going to be in heaven with New America. They would never have to listen to boring babble about the Addendums -- which his fellow Old America Supreme Justice Clarence Thomas often did while fully reclined in his chair facing the heavens with his eyes closed. And, they would never have to discuss them -- which Clarence Thomas was already steadfastly refusing to do because they were so utterly nonsensical[72].

- Second, Scalia reasoned that a country governed with just the original Constitution without any frivolous Addendums would actually be constitutional for the first time in more than two centuries. In other words by "opting out" of Old America and "opting in" to New

---

[72] Once, and only once, a fellow justice asked Justice Thomas why he never debated with lawyers regarding the Addendums like she did. Justice Thomas replied "only a fool argues with an idiot."

America, and Scalia would be fulfilling his oath to "protect and defend" the actual Constitution.

- Third, given that Scalia would be the first and technically only Old America Supreme Court to have completely "checked out" of Old America and into New America, he could be acting Chief Justice for New America.

The Constitution is often suggested to have "three separate yet equal branches," especially by those in the two branches (Congress and Executive) inferior to the "supreme" Court. In actuality, there are three branches and when it all is said and "done" the Supreme court makes the final decisions for all three regarding the Constitution. It is kind of like dividing the whole of government into three parts, with each receiving 33.33% of the responsibility, and the Supreme Court getting the "roundUp."

As with others already living serenely in New America (like Obama on the golf course), Scalia was interested in a nation of villages self-governing peacefully with just the original Constitution. With Scalia's exquisite thinking New America's Supreme Court could effectively retire Old America's Supreme Court, one Justice at a time.

If Scalia really is dead, New America's Supreme Court has zero Justices. If Scalia is alive, however, New America's Supreme Court has just one.

Chalk one up for Scalia :)

32

Conclusion

Since the dawn of civilization people all over the planet have self-organized into villages. Today, voting and taxes are the primary tools villages use to peacefully self-govern. Votes determine how a village manages itself and taxes shape the public policy.

In the case of America, villages are grouped geographically into states. This is true even of villages in the middle of sovereign nations (like the Navajo Nation) and those on islands in the middle of the Pacific ocean (like Hawaii). These states, no matter where now located, are the building blocks of the "United States of America."

Originally, the Constitution for the United States of America enabled all of its citizens to enjoy a wonderful life with the benefits of -

- Every personal liberty imaginable, limited only by "common sense"
- Representatives of the States being chosen by all People (all colors, genders and ages), and
- Taxes being apportioned to the States, not individual people.

The Constitution initially established a strong, resilient, interwoven "democratic republic" to stand the test of time rather than a flimsy democracy that could easily collapse like a house of cards.

Soon after the original Constitution was ratified it was sabotaged with ten onerous amendments addended to it as the Bill of Rights. These oppressive burdens, along with other unwise amendments and Addendums, have made it impossible for America's citizens to live as freely, happily or peacefully as they otherwise would without them. For more than two centuries America's states, villages and citizens have gradually had their rights, freedoms and liberties stripped away, all as a direct consequence of the emasculating, vague, absurd, conflict-causing Constitutional amendments and Addendums.

More concerning, some of the Addendums, particularly "the 17th" which alters the way Senators are selected, have so badly corrupted the structural integrity of America's "democratic republic" it puts the entire federal government at risk of imploding.

On January 1, 2000, the first day of the new year, century and millennium, Cire and other "constitutional purists" bravely commenced upon a journey to save America by starting over with just the original Constitution. The primary objectives were, and remain, to -

- restore all citizens' individual freedoms, liberties and civil rights with common sense
- abolish the federal income tax on people, and
- transition the United States of America from a heavy-hearted "business at war" to an enlightened "government at peace."

When my brother passed away, his friends shared their ongoing collective desire to help transition Old America (unconstitutional and broke with a $14 Trillion deficit) to New America (constitutional and flush with a $14 Trillion surplus). Their suggestion at the time, which is equally true today, was that "the world will be a better place -- happier, friendlier and cleaner -- after Old America is 'swapped out' with New America." The key to accomplishing everything was simply just the original Constitution and "villages, voting and taxes."

My brother sacrificed his life (and family) for his country. May God rest his soul. And, may God bless America.

- The End -

33

Thank you
Twitter and Square

Countless parties helped with Villages Voting & Taxes. Family, friends and neighbors (even Santa Claus and the Easter Bunny!) all provided lots of inspiration for publishing the story. To everyone who helped, "Thank you."

One historically phenomenal company that made many virtually impossible things possible -- like "hacking" the very notion of America -- and deserves special recognition is Twitter. For just over a decade, from January of 2009 (when @ragnaar first started tweeting about unlocking all the characters wrongfully locked up at GITMO for free speech violations) to February of 2019 (when Twitter "locked up" @ragnaar and a bunch of other characters promoting free speech for "free speech violations") Twitter was priceless. Now, unfortunately, an argument can be made that Twitter is virtually worthless, at least when it comes to protecting the rights of people to freely express themselves.

Twitter has four profoundly eloquent and powerful features described below. With just these features -- and without hobbling limitations or xenophobic employees retarding their effectiveness -- Twitter could, and likely would, naturally connect the world's population better than anything else previously available in the public realm.

- **Follow** - The "follow" feature enables a user to follow and read the tweets of other users they choose[73] to follow unless "blocked[74]." Imagine a world where a majority of the population has access to Twitter through their mobile devices, and all are continuously reading and sharing the most timely and relevant information in real time. The result is a global collective consciousness, learning at exponential rates. That was the Twitter I envisioned upon first logging in.

- **Unfollow** - The "unfollow" feature enables a user to instantaneously unfollow another user for whatever reason. There are lots of reasons a user may unfollow another user -- the user "unfollowing" may consider the other user's tweets to be boring, braindead, irrelevant or offensive. In any event, unfollowing enables a user to "eliminate noise" in a twitter timeline. A user can streamline his/her timeline to include only tweets that are most interesting and relevant to that user. In a case

---

[73] Generally, a user may unilaterally choose to follow an account. In some cases where accounts are "locked" or "protected" -- as was the case with @ragnaar -- in order to follow the account a user must first get permission from the account holder.

[74] The "block" function enables a user to prohibit another user from following them. In some ways blocking someone is a bit like using a chainsaw to cut butter -- overkill, and a shame in that it degrades the potential of a pure unlimited collective consciousness.

where a user has more than one interest the user may create more than one twitter timeline with "lists" -- each of which may be precisely refined to feature "clean signal." For example a user interested in religion, politics and Twitter could establish three separate lists, each of which might include world-renowned luminaries on those respective topics. The best minds on the planet, all sharing wisdom in their areas of expertise and collaborating in real-time. Never before was that possible. With twitter it is, or at least it was.

- Reply - The "reply" feature enables a user to reply to another user -- to share ideas and debate the merits of those ideas -- whether they know each other or not. This is an extraordinarily mighty offering. It allows a person to potentially engage in public conversation with any other person in the world.

- Retweet - The "retweet" feature enables a user to "rebroadcast" a tweet to his/her followers, which effectively amplifies the original tweet. When a popular tweet is retweeted by lots of users, the viral effect can be staggering. One simple tweet, successfully retweeted in succession spreads exponentially fast. It's like "rice on a chessboard[75]" except instead of just doubling with each new occurrence, it multiplies by a factor of the user's followers. Theoretically, one tweet could reach

---

[75] In this famous exponential math example, one grain of rice is laid upon the first square of a chessboard and doubled thereafter on each of the 64 squares. One grain, two grains, four grains and so on. In the end, the amount of rice would sufficiently cover all of the land in the world.

every user in the world through retweets in less time than it took to read this sentence.

Despite having so much good going for it, Twitter disappointedly made the same mistake that Old America's federal government began making long ago. It degraded a "frictionless" and scalable system by adding too many counterproductive people and implementing loads of frivolous rules. With each new burdensome person comes a new idea and added pressure to "do something" towards improving an already perfect operating system. With each new rule, what once was nimble becomes sluggish. The result is predictable. Slowly yet inevitably, perfection is incrementally destroyed until the very thing that made Twitter --- and really Old America -- cool in the first place -- vibrant, energetic and enlightened "free speech" -- no longer exists.

A symbolic example may be helpful to consider.

Early on Twitter had a logo designed by a founder of a birdhouse with two holes -- one just big enough for a bird to enter and exit, and another for fresh air and light. A new designer, hired by an assistant to someone in human resources to "improve" the birdhouse logo, eliminated the hole for air and light.

The result? Yes, the logo is simpler. As a consequence, however, the bird enters into a completely dark house and sits in stale air without much light -- kind of like a caveman.

A more practical example may also be helpful to consider.

When Twitter was at its finest, it encouraged its users to be *creative* -- people could improvise, joke and speak freely. Now Twitter encourages, indeed demands, that its users be *cautious*. Otherwise they may be permanently banned from the system, which steadily defeats the preeminent goal of a global collective consciousness through a "chilling of free speech."

Twitter used to be breathtakingly wonderful. It enabled, and benefited from, brilliant "streams of thought" and instantaneous feedback. Now it's bland.

No government or business has ever been successful in censoring or suppressing free speech long term. Twitter won't be the first. Twitter should eliminate its salaried censors, and rely on it's uncompensated users to decide which accounts they want to follow, or not.

As a final note, Twitter's paid tweeps are depressingly duplicitous. Or perhaps more accurately, Twitter's corporate culture doesn't reflect its founders wisdom and compassion. Two of Twitter's founders are highly regarded as vegans, and strive to not kill or consume animals. Another founder has earned great respect for silently meditating long hours contemplating (and presumably now understanding) that the lives of all breathing beings are sacred.

Despite the enlightenment of these founders respecting all life, Twitter has banned accounts advancing the interests of animals, birds and other "breathing beings." Further, Twitter's sometimes ostentatious employees (many of whom are nonetheless otherwise highly regarded for their professional skills) are notorious for routinely devouring the following and then boasting about it with their twitter accounts:

- **Breakfast** - Sliced dead **pig** #LikeMyBaconCrispy

- **Lunch** - Deep fried dead **chicken**.

- **Dinner** - Grilled dead **cow**. Serving as a prime example of stunning self-righteousness sophistry, Twitter's chief international legal guru from India, where cows are worshipped (not hung, drawn and quartered) locked the account of @VotingCow (advancing the notion that cows should live happily rather than be executed).

Bottom line, since God first reportedly provided the commandment to Moses of "thou shall not kill" humans have disobeyed this directive. Collectively humans have massacred and eaten all kinds of living beings -- everything from fish to birds to animals to even other humans. As a general rule, if it has blood and fits on a grill most humans will gobble it up.

It has been this way for as long as most can remember, and may continue indefinitely. But it doesn't have to be forever. With modern-day agriculture which is improving all the time there is now sufficient food on the planet for everyone to eat healthy, delicious and sustaining meals without killing any breathing being.

Let us repeat that here, since we can no longer broadcast it on Twitter without risk of being banned for saying something politically incorrect. There is sufficient food on the planet to feed everyone, without killing any breathing being. In other words, no person should ever starve, or be without food. This is true even if no fish, birds, animals or other breathing beings are prepared as meals.

The world, our collective "Garden of Eden," has sufficient plant-based food resources to provide for everyone. It is just a matter of properly distributing this increasingly plentiful resource to everyone. Eventually, perhaps with the help of Twitter, people will someday realize this and work towards creating highly-efficient small-scale regional agrian zones to feed villagers everywhere with delicious organic food. Until then, hopefully as the enlightenment of the world improves, the slaughters will inversely correlate.

To conclude the thoughts on Twitter, I humbly offer the suggestion that Twitter should strive to follow the lead of its founders and advance the interests of all breathing beings, not just humans who are solely responsible for trashing the planet to the detriment of all. Collectively, all sentient beings share the earth and desire peaceful lives in an environment with clean air and water. This is a goal more easily accomplished with open lines of communication on Twitter -- even for those only able to #chirp.

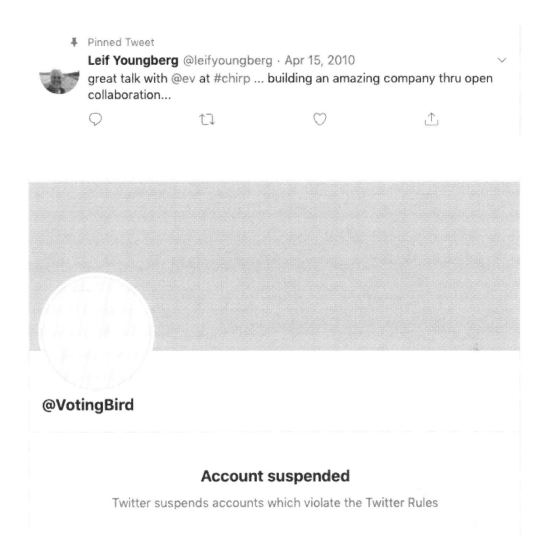

Anyways, a special thanks to Twitter.

After the first "draft" of Villages Voting & Taxes was distributed for review countless readers asked to see a sampling of tweets from accounts that Twitter "locked up" for free speech violations. Some of the tweets, along with a few account summaries, are provided below. Someday, if Twitter ever unlocks the accounts at issue (maybe at the same time the US Government unlocks everybody at GITMO?) additional tweets, ideas and characters will once again be in the public domain.

Another company, closely affiliated with Twitter which was extraordinarily valuable in the process of transitioning Old America to New America is Square. The first "poll tax" for voting in New America was (and all voting since then continues to be) processed with Square. Square likes to promote itself as "making commerce easy." Perhaps even more importantly for villages, Square makes voting and taxes easy.

#ThankYouSquare

Trust For Dogs

@trustfordogs

A Constitutional Voting Trust for Dogs (and all other breathing Beings, sharing clean air, land and water). See @ragnaar. Use @square.

⊙ North America   ⊘ sevenplanet.com

TreeVoting @TreeVoting

All breathing beings ...

#WhatAboutWaterBreathingFish

$\varheartsuit$

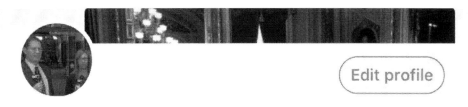

SecondDebate

@ScaliasInHeaven

Fore' Justice Scalia who passed away at a Texas bird ranch with Shotgun & feather pillow over his head contemplating voting rights. See @VotingBird. #UseSquare

⊙ Washington, USA

⦸ c-span.org/video/?441109-...

▦ Joined October 2016

75 Following **26** Followers

Tweets   Tweets & replies   Media   Likes

⚲ Pinned Tweet

SecondDebate @ScaliasIn... · 11/15/17 ⌄
Watergate was an impeachable
offense ...

Cc: @comey @RonWyden
@ChuckGrassley @MikeCrapo

SecondDebate @ScaliasInHe... ·13m ⌄
Scalias #Y2KForkit plan ...

#GoLive c-span.org/video/?452084-...

cc: @VotingBird @senjudiciary

#SpaghettiWarfare
#PlowThroughIt
#AnitaThePinata

Bird @VotingBird · Oct 27

Replying to @VotingApe @KaniksuRocks and 12 others

Just so we are all singing same song ...

"Constitution amended like Animal Farm providing a vote for all eligible

Cc: @votinghippo @jess

VotingHippo LLC

@VotingHippo

Constitutional Wyoming LLC for Hippos and Native Americans orchestrating like kind Treasury swap with @trumpsvolunteer @youngberg23 and @isisofamerica for $FUV

RHINO
@VotingRhino

Credited with seven planet New America roundUps backed with Old America Treasury and square cash tranched for FUV (see @votingape)

Central African Republic

twitter.com/yashar/status/...

Joined September 2017

11 Photos and videos

Tweets	Following	Followers	Likes	Lists	Moments
15	21	5	1	0	0

Tweets   Tweets & replies   Media

Pinned Tweet
RHINO @VotingRhino · Sep 26

Cashed Out

$1

Goat

@VotingGoat

Goat with a vote. Actually a lot of them. Votes for all Goats, via proxy, with @square @twitter and @VotingApe. Roll with #uber.

◎ United States 𝒮 sevenplanet.com

Tweets	Following	Followers	Likes
61	20	5	11

RagnaarFrance
@FranceRagnaar

French Corporation. Tallies things up for
@VotingApe @votingBird and others.
Respect the Vote. Respect the GOAT.

⊙ Paris, France

▦ Joined November 2017

Tweet to RagnaarFrance

🖼 51 Photos and videos

Tweets   Tweets & replies   Media

 RagnaarFrance @FranceRagnaar · Feb 6
twitter.com/hogvoting/stat...

#USTreasuryBlockChain

Cc: @VotingHippo @VotingRhino

#JapaneseCoinHack
#TechHearings
#SatoshiFrance (@criteo)

 VotingHog @HogVoting
twitter.com/trustfordogs/s...

Liquidity pricing rules

TrumpsConstitution @TrumpsV... · 6d ∨
You gonna dunk it ... ?

Gunna throw down a fuckin
tomahawk... :)

Cc: @ChuckGrassley @ragnaar
@SenSchumer

#RevenueNeutral
#DayBreak

Russian Ragnaar 🔒

@RussianRagnaar

Тройной агент. Friends with @ragnaar and @ChinaRagnaar #HackUsForFUV #YesWeDid #4Mo

⊙ Montana, Switzerland   𝒮 sevenplanet.com
◯ Born on December 6, 1965

Edit profile

Ragnaar China ($FUV)

@ChinaRagnaar

七個部落。每個大陸一個。 #HackUsForFUV #CloseGITMO #TrumpGolfAndBeachCuba #NonNegotiable

TrumpsConstitution 🔒

@TrumpsVolunteer Follows you

Trumps Volunteer helping reorganize US (after National Bankruptcy - see usdebtclock.org). #CloseGitmo. Use @Square. Refi with @SoFi.

What's happening?

TrumpsConstitution 🔒
@TrumpsVolunteer

Tweets	Following	Followers
403	43	7

Portland trends · Change

#BAONPDX
1,509 Tweets

#NWSL
1,085 Tweets

#MondayMotivation
126K Tweets

#TreasonSummit
398K Tweets

#PrimeDay
21.6K Tweets

Helsinki
286K Tweets

Trump and Putin
President Trump meets Russian president
Vladimir Putin in Finland

JUST ANNOUNCED
9,576 Tweets

Mark Knoller ✔ @markknoller · 5m
Setting up for Trump/Putin joint press conference on conclusion of their talks.

💬 1   ↻ 10   ♡ 13   ✉

TrumpsConstitution 🔒 @TrumpsVolunteer · 11s
чистый воздух
реки с чистой водой, чтобы выпить
гольф-россия

cc: @RussianGolfHack

💬   ↻   ♡   ᵢₗᵢ

216

@TrumpsVolunteer
@TrumpsVolunteer

Account suspended

Twitter suspends accounts that violate the
Twitter Rules.

NotRealDonaldTrump @SantaClausTrump · 31 Oct 2017

We support free speech
within reason

Cc: @ISIS_Mohammad @senjudiciary @ragnaar @ISISofAmerica @ISIS_Florida
@google @twitter
#TechHearings

RUSSIA & 2016 ELECTION INVESTIGATIONS
SEAN EDGETT
Twitter
Acting General Counsel

NoStandingArmy

@ISIS_Florida

Radical Muslims, Christians and Jews - All Friends & Loyalists who have sworn to Protect and Defend the Constitution. Join us and vote! #CloseGitmo #UseSquare

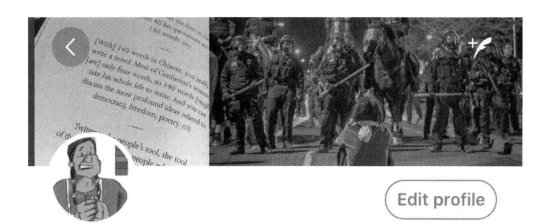

johngalt008 🔒

@johngalt008

"New America" Character established when @twitter "locked" @ragnaar based on Atlas Shrugged (see @RussianGolfHack with @ChinaRagnaar) #HackUsForFUV

🔗 abqjournal.com/apd-under-fire...

📅 Joined March 2009

Edit profile

ragnaar ✓
@ragnaar

#SaintScalia

📍 kaniksu

📅 Joined January 2009

📷 910 Photos and videos

TWEETS	FOLLOWING	FOLLOWERS	LIKES	LISTS
54.5K	52	10	134	3

Edit profile

Tweets   Tweets & replies   Media

ragnaar @ragnaar ✓ · 10 Sep 2014
the 500 year plan ... 'let country try its best for 250 years ... and then try again ... and again ...
usdebtclock.org

34

Afterwards

The last time Cire called was a few days after my wife left for the Sioux Territory (part of the Louisiana Purchase, later remapped as North Dakota) to take care of her deathly-ill Dad who, unfortunately, had since died.

He said he had "lots" of good updates.

First, he confirmed that he was, of course, not dead.

He did feel like he was dead though. He was in China. The wall was nice but the air in the cities was so polluted it was difficult to "berieve" (Chinese slang for "breathe" or maybe "believe").

Second, he mentioned that he had recently upgraded from a Canadian Blackberry to a Chinese iPhone, a simply superior smartphone, and suggested that I do the same. His blackberries were all being retired and slated to be featured in a hilarious movie. He relayed that one reason for ditching the Blackberries was that a pair of Canadian Mounties had

hacked into our private family communications -- a key "black binder" with "non-negotiable" instructions from the Global Settlement for returning Canada back to the Native Americans. He then suggested with a cheerful sense of promise that both characters should be sent to GITMO on behalf of the Human Rights Museum in Winnipeg. There they could set free the Muslim ragheads (represented by @ragnaar, a depiction of the prophet Mohammad) being tortured for saying scary things in Arabic -- and help convert Guantanamo Bay to a Trump Beach and Golf Resort©.

Third, and most surprisingly, he shared that Dad was not dead. Yet, he was in "heaven." The country club "voters" (all golfers paying a recurring membership fee nicknamed "the hackers poll tax") had elected him a while back to "play god" and given him "carte blanche" to execute his will.

His first order of business had been to "reverse course." The country club had featured the same layout for the last century with the golfers striving to drive into the fairway towards the mountains in the East at the first tee. Every single morning like clockwork at least one golfer would "break the silence" by complaining, joking or simply stating they were "blinded with light" from the sun.

Dad changed up everything to "keep the peace and quiet" with a masterful swap. Now, instead of teeing off in the morning staring directly at the sun, you teed off with the sun comfortably on your back. Dad had "reversed the nines." Hole 1 was now Hole 10. And, of course, 10 was now 1.

It got even better though. Based on the overwhelming success of the improvements to the country club ("on time" and "under budget"), Dad was asked to redesign the University Championship Golf course where he had scored his back-to-back "eagles" on 9/11. For this course he was given a "blank check[76]."

---

[76] For processing *either* by (i) Old America's Federal Reserve noted for an *infinite* supply of "petro dollars" made up from thin air and currently spread across the planet like pollution, or (ii) New America's Treasury bank with a *finite* reserve of "roundUps." Like gold and silver (the two precious metals named in the Constitution), the universe has only a fixed amount of roundUps.

He once again completely changed the direction of everything, yet even more radically.

He replaced "all the greens" with "gold markers[77] (for tee boxes) -- and drained the swamp. Now golfers marched towards "new greens" where the gold markers previously were. The former final green (the "18th" where Dad had scored his finishing "eagle" on 9/11, the one next to the clubhouse where Dad's memorial services were held), was now where the professionals first teed things up.

Bottom line, Dad was happy, healthy and still young, golfing in the 70's.

Cire could accurately report on all this as he had just finished a round of golf with Dad in China, where Dad had nailed a 1-iron.

Captain America 🔒
@RalphCYoungberg

driver ... red ... truck ... breaker ... one ... nine ...

Joined September 2014

Cire then joked that since Dad was even better than God ('cause not even God can hit a 1-iron), that he (Cire) was even better than God's second son.

---

[77] The course has four tee boxes (Gold, Blue, White and Red) to start each hole. The "gold markers" are "farthest from the green."

Then, dead seriously, he relayed that my wife, who had not attended my Dad's funeral and later stormed out of Cire's "Celebration of Life" services in dramatic fashion, was pretty much behind everything. She had perfectly engaged with Cire on his last visit to our "Garden of Eden" for a modern era biblical story of the "second coming of God's son." And she, being the family expert in communication, had even written Cire's "Political View" (featured in Chapter 2).

When I confided to him that my wife's participation in the "fake news" of his death had soured our marriage and effectively ruined my sons' childhoods, he cold-heartedly reminded me of how my wife had summed up his Political View with the conclusion that "participation ... is worth the sacrifice." In other words, my wife was helping transition Old America to New America at the expense of our family.

Then, in classic no nonsense form, Cire texted me his twitter account summary and a "consolidated accounting" for Old America and New America. Cire's Master Plan to "Shred the Amendments" and "start over with just the original Constitution," which at one time had been dismissed by non-believers as pure fantasy, was now reality -- at least in our peaceful village of America and the surrounding lands.

Cire Grebgnuoy
@EricYoungberg

Dead white politician credited with relentless logic helping @potus persuade parties of wisdom of following just Original Constitution #ShredTheAmendments

📍 #kaniksu

📅 Joined June 2010

Master Plan for America
('00 to '20)

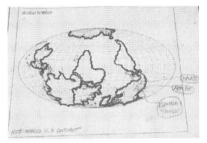

Goals

- **Air** clean enough to breathe
- Rivers with **Water** clean enough to drink
- Nourishing **Food** For All
- **Peace** on Earth (or at least within the villages)

Reserves	
New America Treasury	14 Trillion
Operations	
Village Voluntary Taxes	100,000
Road Less Traveled	TBD
Balance Available	100,000
Voting	
Poll Taxes (Less Fees)	0.64

Made in the USA
Middletown, DE
25 May 2020